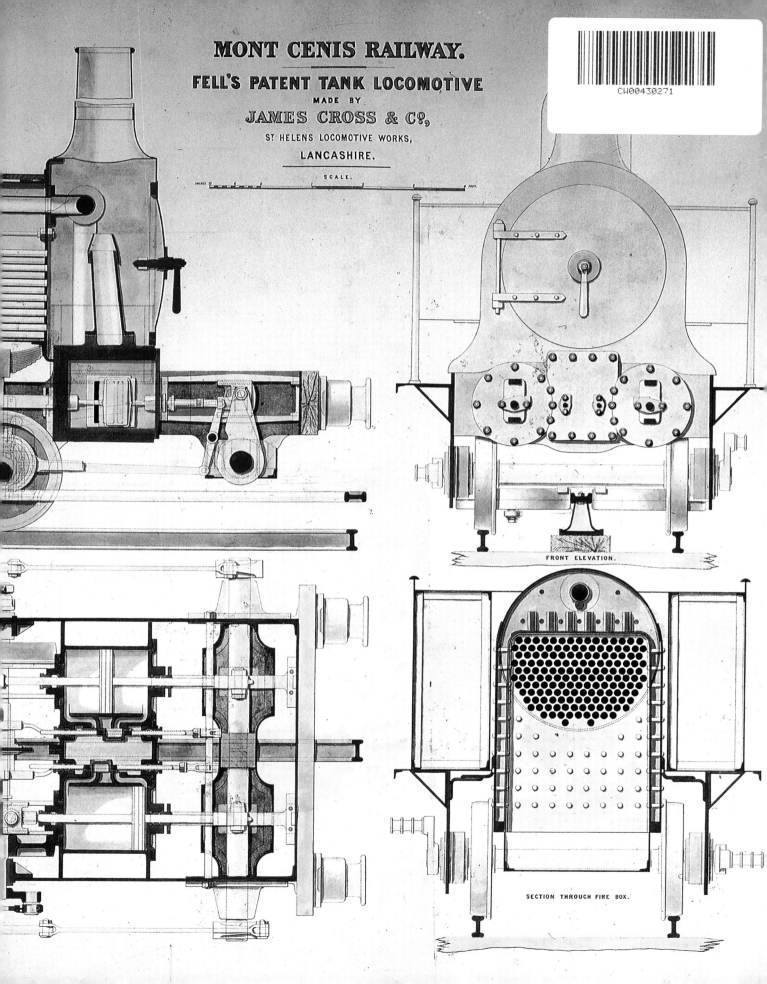

# MONT CENIS RAILWAY.

## FELL'S PATENT TANK LOCOMOTIVE

MADE BY

### JAMES CROSS & Cᵒ,

ST HELENS LOCOMOTIVE WORKS,

LANCASHIRE.

SCALE.

FRONT ELEVATION.

SECTION THROUGH FIRE BOX.

# THE
# MONT CENIS
# FELL RAILWAY

*The Mont Cenis Fell Railway, a contemporary print. The train is ascending by zig-zags to the col from Lanslebourg, which can be seen in the valley to the right. Running along the edge of the road, it has overtaken a horsedrawn diligence which can be seen in the lower right hand corner, and will turn back on itself to follow the road which can be seen, top left.*

**Le Chemin de Fer du Mont Cenis, gravure d'époque.** *Le train zigzague pour monter vers le col, après avoir quitté Lanslebourg qu'on peut voir dans la vallée à droite. Il avance le long de la route, ayant dépassé une diligence visible en bas à droite, puis il fera demi-tour pour suivre la route qu'on voit en haut à gauche.*
Musées d'Art et d'Histoire de Chambéry.

# THE
# MONT CENIS
# FELL RAILWAY

BY

P. J. G. RANSOM

TWELVEHEADS PRESS

TRURO 1999

*By the same author*

Holiday Cruising in Ireland

Railways Revived

Waterways Restored

Your Book of Canals

The Archaeology of Canals

The Archaeology of Railways

Your Book of Steam RailwayPreservation

The Archaeology of the Transport Revolution 1750-1850

Transport in Scotland through the Ages

The Victorian Railway and How It Evolved

Scottish Steam Today

Loch Earn

Narrow Gauge Steam: Its origins and world-wide development

Scotland's Inland Waterways

**TWELVEHEADS PRESS**

First published 1999 by Twelveheads Press.
Chy Mengleth, Twelveheads, Truro, Cornwall TR4 8SN.
ISBN 0 906294 41 X
British Library Cataloguing-in-Publication Data.
A catalogue record for this book is available from the British Library.
Designed by Alan Kittridge. Printed by The Amadeus Press Ltd., Huddersfield.

# CONTENTS

*This oil station lamp was among the MCR equipment acquired by the Lausanne-Echallens Railway - as was discovered when, in the 1960s, layers of old paint were removed to reveal the oval MCR plate.*
**Cette lanterne à pétrole, faisant partie de l'équipement du Chemin de Fer du Mont Cenis acquis par le Chemin de Fer Lausanne-Echallens, fut découverte dans les années 60, époque à laquelle la plaque ovale fut révélée sous plusieurs couches de peinture.**
CREDIT: SEE ACKNOWLEDGEMENTS.

## INTRODUCTORY NOTES

At the period when the Mont Cenis Railway was built and operated (1866-72) photography of railways was still uncommon - despite, for instance, the interest aroused by the introduction of steam locomotives on the Festiniog Railway in 1863, the earliest known photographs of it date only from the 1870s. The MCR did attract the attention of photographers, happily, and many of the results appear here, even though their quality, in some instances, would not be good enough to merit reproduction were a recent period represented. Regrettably but inevitably they include no photographs of moving trains, as such photography did not become practicable until the 1880s.

One of the remarkable features to emerge from researching the story of the Mont Cenis Railway was the facility with which the people concerned could switch between imperial and metric units, and back again, even within the same document. Clearly they were at home with both systems: there was no nonsense then about consistency or equivalents! Here I have tended to leave units as I found them, quoting for instance the gauge of the railway as 1.10 metres rather than 3 feet 7$^5$/$_{16}$ inches, but I have inserted equivalents, one way or the other, where they seemed essential.

## LE CHEMIN DE FER DU MONT CENIS - SOMMAIRE EN FRANCAIS

Vers les années 1860, le seul point noir dans la ligne ferrée entre Brindisi/Calais se situait entre Suse et Saint Michel de Maurienne. Un tunnel de 12 kilomètres était bien en construction mais sa realisation devait s'étaler sur plusieurs années. Les passagers voyageaient donc par diligence ou en traineau par le col du Mont Cenis à une altitude atteignant 2.081 mètres.

Ceci préoccupait le gouvernement britannique qui souhaitait accélérer l'acheminement du courrier en provenance d'Inde en le déviant par Brindisi plutòt que par Marseille. Cette situation était également bien connue du constructeur de chemins de fer brittanique réputé, Thomas Brassey et de son partenaire John Barraclough Fell. Thomas Brassey avait déjà réalisé plusieurs lignes en France et en Italie. Fell proposa la construction d'une ligne provisoire parallèle à la route du Mont Cenis. Pour gravir des rampes encore jamais vues à 83‰, les locomotives devaient être équipèes de roues motrices supplémentaires, positionnées à l'horizontale afin suivre un rail central situé entre ces dernières.

Après plusieurs tentatives, une compagnie britannique vit le jour et les gouvernements français et italien accordèrent la concession de la ligne de chemin de fer jusqu'à l'ouverture du tunnel. Les promoteurs du projet tablaient sur 7 années d'exploitation pour atteindre la rentabilité. Malgré de nombreux imprévus pendant la construction, le chemin de fer du Mont Cenis fut ouvert en juin 1868, les locomotives et le matériel roulant furent construits en France.

Pendant les 26 premiers mois d'exploitation, les trains parcourirent plus de 321.000 kilomètres, transporterent plus de 100.000 passagers, des marchandises et du courrier. Après l'introduction d'une machinerie à air comprimé, les travaux concernant le tunnel avancèrent à un rythme plus rapide que prévu: le tunnel fut ouvert en octobre 1871 alors que le chemin de fer du Mont Cenis n'était opérationnel que depuis 3 ans et 4 mois. Une grande partie du matériel roulant alla au chemin de fer reliant Lausanne à Echallens en Suisse, où un wagon du chemin de fer du Mont Cenis restauré participe maintenant à des manifestations spéciales de machines à vapeur. Par ailleurs, à côté de la route au-dessus du Mont Cenis, il est encore possible de voir ce nos jours les tunnels et abris anti-avalanche construits à l'époque pour protéger la ligne provisoire.

## LA FERROVIA DEL MONCENISIO - RIASSUNTO IN ITALIANO

Nel secolo scorso, verso la metà degli anni sessanta, l'unico collegamento mancante nella linea ferroviaria da Brindisi - nel tallone della penisola Italiana - a Calais - dirimpetto all'Inghilterra - era costituito dal tratto compreso tra Susa e St Michel de Maurienne. Allora erano già stati avviati i lavori per la costruzione di un tunnel della lunghezza di 12 chilometri nelle Alpi: ma il completamento di questo progetto avrebbe richiesto diversi anni. Nel frattempo i passeggeri dovevano viaggiare in diligenza o attraversare il Passo del Moncenisio in slitta, raggiungendo altitudini di 2.081 metri.

Ciò preoccupava il governo Britannico, interessato ad accelerare il servizio di corrispondenza postale proveniente dall'India, dirottandolo attraverso Brindisi anzichè Marsiglia. Sia il rinomato appaltatore ferroviario inglese, Thomas Brassey, che aveva costruito numerose ferrovie in Italia ed in Francia, che il suo socio John Baraclough Fell conoscevano perfettamente la situazione. Fell propose quindi la costruzione di una linea ferroviaria temporanea, costeggiante la strada del Moncenisio. Per arrampicarsi su inclinazioni dell'83‰, pendenze senza precedenti, le locomotive avrebbero dovuto essere munite di ruote motrici accessorie, collocate orizzontalmente affinchè potessero far presa su di un binario centrale situato nel loro mezzo.

Dopo varie sperimentazioni, fu fondata una società Britannica alla quale il governo Francese e quello Italiano diede l'autorizzazione per la costruzione della ferrovia con una concessione valida sino all'apertura del tunnel. I fondatori della società calcolarono che ai fini del rendimento di un buon utile dall'operazione, sarebbero stati necessari sette anni. La costruzione presentò diversi problemi imprevisti, ma la Ferrovia del Moncenisio venne infine aperta nel giungo del 1868. La fabbricazione dei materiali rotabili e della locomotive avvenne in Francia.

Durante i primi due anni e tre mesi di attività della ferrovia, vennero percorsi con successo più di 320.000 chilometri da treni per il trasporto di più di 100.000 passeggeri, merci e posta. Tuttavia, in seguito all'introduzione dei macchinari di trivellazione ad aria compressa, il tunnel venne terminato molto prima del previsto: se ne inaugurò l'apertura nell'ottobre del 1871 quando la Ferrovia del Moncenisio aveva solamente tre anni e quattro mesi di vita. Gran parte dei suoi materiali rotabili venne destinata al tratto ferroviario Losanna-Echalense in Svizzera; dove una carrozza ferroviaria della Ferrovia del Moncenisio, dopo i dovuti restauri, va ancora a tutto vapore e, accanto alla strada che percorre il Moncenisio, si possono vedere tuttora i tunnel ed i luoghi di riparo dalle valanghe costruiti in tempi tanto lontani per l'attuale ferrovia.

# CHAPTER ONE
# THE PASS ITSELF

The Mont Cenis Fell Railway: lest there be any misapprehension, Fell in this context is not a hill, nor a hillside, but a person - John Barraclough Fell, 1815-1902. Yet it is strangely fortuitous that this surname, associated originally with residence by high ground, should have been borne by the first man to make steam trains climb mountains. His contemporaries, Sylvester Marsh in America and Niklaus Riggenbach in Switzerland, had similar ambitions and would use the rack-and-pinion system to achieve success; in Fell's system the locomotives had additional driving wheels, which were horizontal and gripped a central rail which passed between them. This arrangement provided adhesion far greater than could result from a locomotive's weight alone. The principle was not new (no more was rack-and-pinion) but Fell was first to make it a practical success. The Mont Cenis Railway reached an altitude of 6,828 feet above sea level by means of gradients as steep as 1 in 12; when it was opened in 1868 Fell had made a practical success of the mountain railway too (even though Marsh and Riggenbach would not be far behind). At that date railways and railway engineering were still young. To contemporaries the Mont Cenis Railway was astonishing: nothing like it had been seen before.

But what is Mont Cenis, and where, and what was Fell doing there? If Fell in the title is open to misunderstanding, so too is Mont Cenis, for this is not a single mountain but a *massif*, a group of mountains which form part of the spine of the southern Alps separating France from Italy. What we are concerned with here is not so much the mountains themselves, but the *Col du Mont Cenis* which provides a pass through them and links the two countries. (In case there are still further misunderstandings, Mont Cenis is not in Switzerland, despite at least one recent railway book which suggested that it was in that country.)

As an international link for long-distance traffic, the pass has long since been superseded by tunnels for both road and rail which burrow far beneath the ridge. The railway tunnel was the first great Alpine tunnel, but so limited were tunnelling techniques when work commenced in 1857 that it was expected to be many years, perhaps decades, before it was complete. Hence the scheme for a railway over the top, purely as a temporary expedient.

So the Mont Cenis Pass is now little known, a backwater of communications. Travellers who do seek it out discover a classic Alpine pass, its road approach from either side a series of ferocious zig-zags. Even today, to build any sort of railway following this road would be a formidable undertaking. To build one in the 1860s, in the aftermath of a financial crash, against a background of wars and the threat of wars, and to plan to take eighteen months to do so, for an intended life of seven years, with operation dependent on new technology untried in practice - this was an enterprise of quite staggering boldness.

*In 1995 a sign advises walkers that they have reached the 'Tunnel Fell'. It is in fact a masonry avalanche shelter, where the railway started its descent into Italy.*
*En 1995 un panneau indique aux randonneurs qu'ils ont atteint le Tunnel Fell. C'est en fait une construction en maçonnerie permettant de s'abriter des avalanches.*
AUTHOR.

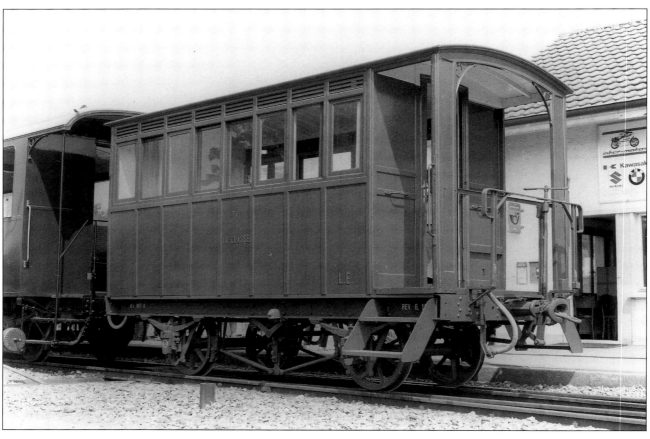

*A reconstructed Mont Cenis Railway coach runs in a steam special on the Lausanne-Echallens-Bercher Railway in 1982.*
**Un voiture du Chemin de Fer du Mont Cenis attaché à un train à vapeur special de la ligne Lausanne-Echallens-Bercher en 1982.**
CREDIT: SEE ACKNOWLEDGEMENTS.

It was Victorian commercial Britain at its most ebullient. For it was indeed a British enterprise - promoted in Britain, laid out by British engineers, operated by a British company. It attracted the most distinguished Britons, connected with railways, of the day. The Duke of Sutherland, Thomas Brassey and Capt. Henry Tyler were among those concerned in addition to Fell himself. What they achieved was an engineering triumph - and if they did not reap the hoped-for financial rewards, this was due not so much to shortcomings of its own, although it was not devoid of these, as to developments elsewhere which were largely unforeseeable. Furthermore, on this railway which was intended for so limited a life, they built so soundly that substantial traces remain to be seen in the 1990s, while some of its rolling stock, transferred to the Lausanne-Echallens-Bercher Railway, survived in use until the 1960s and to this day a restored Mont Cenis

Railway coach continues on occasion to be included in the LEB's summer Sunday steam specials.

To find out why all this should have been so, it is necessary to look into the earlier history of the pass - and indeed of Italy itself, despite the risk of over-simplifying a subject of immense complexity.

Since the decline of the Roman Empire, Italy had consisted of a multitude of independent states and cities. Savoy, west of the Alps, was not then part of France but was one of these Italian states. By the mid-eighteenth century the Dukes of Savoy had acquired Sardinia and with it the title King of Sardinia; their kingdom included also Piedmont, contiguous with Savoy but east of the Alps, and their capital was at Turin.

The Napoleonic period between 1796 and 1814 brought the whole of Italy under French domination; Piedmont and Savoy were

8

absorbed into France itself. With the defeat of Napoleon, however, the Congress of Vienna gave north-eastern Italy, that is Venetia and Lombardy, to Austria. Otherwise the old rulers returned, but throughout most of Italy Austrian influence became dominant. The Kingdom of Sardinia, including Piedmont, Savoy, Nice and Genoa, became at British insistence a buffer state between Austria and France.

In the rest of Italy, Austrian domination seemed scarcely more welcome than French. There began the *Risorgimento*, that is to say the movement which would lead eventually to unification of Italy as an independent state, but an attempt to drive the Austrians out of north Italy in 1848-9, the first war of independence, was a failure.

By 1852 the kingdom of Sardinia was (unusually in Italy) a constitutional monarchy, under a young king, Victor Emmanuel II, with a new premier, Count Camillo Cavour. Cavour was strong-willed, fair-minded, friendly towards Britain and France and aiming for another war with Austria. In this he found a willing ally in Napoleon III, emperor of France and nephew of Napoleon Bonaparte; but in return for help in driving Austria out of Italy Napoleon wanted the cession of Savoy and Nice to France.

It was Austria which eventually declared war in the spring of 1859; the French arrived in Italy, fought and won two battles (Magenta and Solferino) and then, since Napoleon had been keener on the war than his countrymen were, made peace. Lombardy, Tuscany and most other north Italian states were joined with Piedmont. But in 1860, following a plebiscite, Savoy and Nice did become French, and the Austrians still held Venetia. Otherwise, Italy was united in 1861, with the principal exceptions of Venetia and Rome itself, which was still under Papal rule. Victor Emmanuel was proclaimed king and Britain was first to recognise the new kingdom. The following June, Cavour died. It was at this point in history that the railway over the Mont Cenis was projected, in 1862.

The opportunity for Italy to acquire Venetia arose in 1865: Prussia, under Bismarck, anticipated war with Austria and sought Italy as an ally in order to divide the Austrian army. War was declared in June 1866. From the Italian point of view it was a war of incompetent command and indecisive battles, and when peace was signed in October it seems to have been due as much as anything to Napoleon III's diplomacy that Venetia became part of the Italian kingdom. To take the story to the end of the Mont Cenis Railway period, Rome after many difficulties and some fighting joined the rest of Italy in 1870. Elsewhere in 1870-1 the Franco-Prussian war brought the defeat of France and the downfall of Napoleon III.

Throughout this long history the Col du Mont Cenis was, despite its altitude and the steepness of its approaches, the principal route between France and Italy (its main rival was travel by sea along the Mediterranean coast). Hannibal crossed the Mont Cenis with his army and his elephants in Roman times, the Emperor Frederick Barbarossa did so with his armies several times in the twelfth century.

In the eighteenth century innumerable notable Britons on the Grand Tour crossed over the Mont Cenis. Many of them (Horace Walpole, Edward Gibbon, James Boswell, for instance) wrote of it, and the pass became famous, indeed notorious, in Britain. Walpole, in its approaches, had the misfortune to have his spaniel seized by a wolf. On the pass itself, winter snow lay deep for months on end, and even in summer travellers found that no carriage road crossed it. At Lanslebourg on the Savoy side, and at Novalesa on the Piedmont side (for the border ran generally along the ridge) carriages were dismantled, and their components were carried across by mules. The traveller, seated on a sort of litter, was carried higher than he had ever experienced, over steep and precipitous paths by sure-footed porters. In winter snows the same sure-footed porters dragged him, or her, uphill on a sledge and then, on the Lanslebourg side, steered it downhill in next to no time. This predecessor of the Cresta Run was regarded with horror by all except apparently the English, who were inclined to go back up to the top and do it all over again for fun! But although the pass was a very dangerous crossing in winter, on a clear summer day its plateau, where Alpine meadows and a little lake were surrounded by high peaks, was a delight.

There had been thoughts of building a carriage road over the Mont Cenis pass as early as the end of the seventeenth century, but it was only in the Napoleonic period that such a road became reality. It was laid out by Dausse, chief engineer of Isère Departement and construction commenced in 1803. From Lanslebourg to the summit this road (the existence of which was vital to the later Fell railway) climbed steadily through a series of zig-zags with five hairpin bends. On the Piedmont side the road avoided plunging straight down to Novalesa, descending by comparison gradually along the flanks of the hills to reach the valley bottom at the town of Susa. The total width of the road was 10 metres, of which the central six metres were metalled.

By 1805 works were far enough advanced for light vehicles to cross the Mont Cenis without being dismantled; it was 1808 before the road was opened to all traffic. At intervals along it, twenty five refuges were built in which blizzard-stranded travellers might take shelter, and the hospice on the plateau, which had been closed down, was re-established. The road approach to Lanslebourg, up the valley known as the Maurienne, had also been much improved, and together these roads became part of the 'Route impériale de première classe de Paris à Milan'.

The road certainly met a need, for as early as 1811 it was noted that 17,000 vehicles had crossed the pass in that year. Of these, 14,000 were goods vehicles; there were in addition 45,000 pack animals. A service of diligences was established between Lyons and Turin: the diligence, drawn by four or six horses, was the French equivalent of the stage coach, although

*How travellers crossed Mont Cenis in the eighteenth century.*
**Un voyageur traversant le Mont Cenis au 18ème siècle.**
COPYRIGHT © BRITISH MUSEUM.

a larger vehicle. The word is a contraction of *carosse de diligence*, or fast coach, for *diligence*, in French, signifies not only effort but also speed.

Travel by diligence was well described by the mountaineer Edward Whymper in his book *Scrambles amongst the Alps*.... He was writing about the early 1860s when, despite the approach of railways either side of the Mont Cenis, diligences still provided the link over it:

> The diligence service was excellent... The horses were changed as rapidly as on the best lines in the best period of coaching in England... When the zig-zags began, teams of mules were hooked on, and the driver and his helpers marched by their side... Passengers dismounted, and stretched their legs by cutting the curves. The pace was slow but steady, and scarcely a halt was made during the rise of 2,000 feet... The summit was gained, the mules were detached... we with fresh horses were dragged at the gallop over the plain to the other side...
>
> The air was keen and often chilly, but the summit was soon passed, and one quickly descended to warmth again. Once more there was a change. The horses, reduced in number to three, or perhaps two, were the sturdiest and most sure of foot, and they raced down with the precision of old stagers... the conductor ...screwed down the breaks as the corners were approached. The horses, held well in hand, leant inwards as the top-heavy vehicle, so suddenly checked, heeled almost over; but in another moment the break was released, and again they swept down, urged onwards by...the driver.

To cross the pass in winter, coach bodies were mounted on sledge runners. But all this was changed, as Whymper remarked, by construction of the Fell railway.

CHAPTER TWO

# THROUGH A TUNNEL, OR OVER THE TOP?

The steam railway was invented in Britain, but British engineers, financiers and railway contractors were soon at work on the Continent. Among the earliest was Thomas Brassey (1805-1870) whose tender for construction of the Paris & Rouen Railway, the first main line in France, was accepted in 1841. Brassey, who eventually became the most noted of all Victorian railway contractors, had come into the business by supplying building stone to George Stephenson for the Liverpool & Manchester Railway and then contracting to build part of the Grand Junction. A combination of honest dealing and accurate pricing, at a period when neither was particularly commonplace among his fellows, enabled him to build up a business which became world-wide: he was responsible for construction, eventually, of nearly 4,500 miles of railway.

Despite enormous financial risk - Brassey's wages bill alone was at one period £20,000 a week - almost all of this had been achieved without, in the manner of the time, the benefit of limited liability. Railway contractors did spread their risks a little by working in partnerships; the composition of these changed from contract to contract with bewildering frequency. Quite often work is attributed simply to 'Brassey & Co.' (or, in France, to *la Compagnie Brassey*).

Two other Englishmen who were involved with railways in France at this early stage, and who would eventually be associated with Brassey at Mont Cenis, were William Buddicom and Edward Blount. William Barber Buddicom (1816-1887) had been a resident engineer on the Liverpool & Manchester and then locomotive superintendent of the Grand Junction. In 1841 he grasped the opportunity to set up Allcard, Buddicom & Co. in France, to build locomotives for the Paris & Rouen Railway,

and to work the line by contract. From that start he soon became associated with many other main lines built in France over the next decade.

Finance for the Paris & Rouen had been raised partly in Britain, partly in France, and closely involved on the French side was the young Englishman, Edward Blount (1809-1905), who had set up a finance house in Paris. Sensing the opportunities offered by railways, Blount had thought it as well to gain a thorough understanding of them by working for four months on the footplate of locomotives on the London & Birmingham Railway. When losses caused by the revolution of 1848 ruined him, it was Brassey and Buddicom who provided the financial support to set him up in business again - such involvement of contractors in finance was becoming increasingly common at home and abroad. In 1864 Blount became chairman of the Western Railway of France.

As the backbone of the railway system in Britain approached completion around 1850, financiers, engineers and contractors turned their attention increasingly abroad. Italy was to prove fruitful ground. Robert Stephenson was engineer-in-chief for the Leghorn-Florence line; Brunel was consulted over the line from Genoa to Turin (he recommended 4 feet 8½ inches gauge). It was the first in Piedmont, opened between 1848 and 1853. Brassey and his associates, according to figures extracted from Helps's biography, were responsible for construction, between 1850 and 1865, of 546 miles of Italian railways in eight different contracts.

This was the formative period for development of the Italian railway system, but its story is as complex if not more so than the complex political history of Italy at the period - railways were divided up and amalgamated into other railway undertakings according to the changing national allegiances of the territories they served.

Development of railways in Piedmont was greatly assisted by the advocacy of Cavour, by substantial investment by government and contractors, and by authorisation through government concessions at a cost to the promoters which was minimal compared to the heavy Parliamentary costs suffered by railway promoters in Britain. During the 1850s Brassey and various partners were responsible for a route which extended from Culoz, where the River Rhône formed the frontier between France and Savoy, by Chambéry and Susa to Turin and onward, in the direction of Milan, to Buffalora where the River Ticino formed the frontier between Piedmont and Austrian territory. In this route there was a break, to which we will return shortly, at Mont Cenis: from St Jean de Maurienne to Susa traffic continued to use the road over the pass. The whole rail route formed the Victor Emmanuel Railway, which built the section in Savoy and absorbed the Piedmont sections. In addition to the commercial importance of this route, which linked with the earlier Genoa-Turin railway, its strategic importance is evident in the build-up to war between France and Austria.

Also of importance at this period was construction of the Central Italian Railway which by connecting earlier lines provided a route from Milan to Bologna and Florence. For the 52-mile section over the Apennine Mountains between Bologna and Pistoia, a contract was awarded in 1854 to a partnership of T. Brassey, W. Jackson, J. B. Fell and C. M. Jopling.

J. B. Fell, although born in London, came from an old Furness family, and had accompanied his parents when they returned to Furness in the 1830s. Here he worked among other things in the family timber business, with sawmill and slipway at Greenodd. Fell was also a leading light in the Windermere Steam Yacht Company, which placed the paddle steamer *Lady of the Lake* in service on Lake Windermere in 1845 - the first steamer to operate there. Towards the end of the 1840s the railway age had belatedly

reached Furness, and J. B. Fell in partnership with C. M. Jopling contracted to build railways which were, or would become, part of the Furness Railway's system. Jopling had earlier worked under Brassey on construction of the Kendal & Windermere Railway, built between 1845 and 1847; Fell probably first came into contact with Brassey at that period. By 1852, however, Fell and Jopling were in Italy building the Genoa & Voltri Railway. On the Central Italian contract, the fourth partner, William Jackson, was already associated with Brassey in other ventures, notably the Victor Emmanuel Railway.

On the Bologna-Pistoia line, Fell and Jopling were not only partners but also the agents on the spot. The mountain section, called the Poretta Inclines, included innumerable tunnels and viaducts. Its ruling gradient was 1 in 40, achieved by a sinuous course with frequent 15-chain curves. This increased the $15^{1}/_{2}$ miles by road, between its extremities at Pistoia and Poretta, to some 25 miles by rail. It must have been abundantly clear to Fell that, if the ruling gradient could have been increased, the route length, the cost, and the time for construction could all have been reduced.

Indeed the point may have made itself evident even earlier, for when resident in Furness in the late 1830s he must have been aware of the controversy over the route to be taken by the main Anglo-Scottish railway: whether, as favoured by George Stephenson, it should take a near-level but very circuitous route following the coast, or whether as favoured by Joseph Locke (and eventually built by Brassey) it should follow the shorter but steeper route over Shap. But Shap summit is a mere 914 feet above sea level, and was attained by a ruling grade of 1 in 75. Clearly, railway-building in the mountains of Italy offered a much greater challenge than anything usual at home. The Turin-Genoa line already incorporated the $6^{1}/_{4}$-mile Giovi Incline which averaged 1 in 38 and included a stretch of 1 in $28^{1}/_{2}$. In general, 1 in 25 was considered the steepest gradient practicable for a railway.

Fell's travels took him many times over the

Mont Cenis pass. The railway from Turin was opened to Susa in 1854 and, on the western side, the railway from Culoz reached St Jean de Maurienne in 1856. To close the gap, the intended solution was to tunnel beneath the mountain range. Indeed there had been proposals for tunnels during the 1840s. Work eventually commenced in 1857 on a tunnel which was to be 12,220 metres (13,364 yards) long and, for double track, 8 m wide and 7 m high. It was a colossal project: Sir Cusack Roney was to point out in 1868[1] that, at over 7$^1$/$_2$ miles long, it was 4$^1$/$_2$ miles longer than the next longest railway tunnel in Europe. And in 1857 tunnelling machinery still lay in the future: the builders had only hand labour to work with, and gunpowder for blasting. Furthermore, the great depth of the tunnel beneath the mountain range meant that no intermediate shafts were practicable: the tunnel could be driven, and ventilated, only from the ends. The Savoy end was situated at Fourneaux close to Modane, and the Piedmont end at Bardonèccia. It did not, therefore, pass directly beneath Mont Cenis, although sometimes known by that name; it is more correctly known as the Fréjus Tunnel or, to contemporaries of its construction, 'the great tunnel of the Alps'. Progress was exceptionally slow: during the first few years, it averaged, at the Bardonèccia end, 0.64 metres a day, and at the Fourneaux end only 0.5 metres.

Accounts of how the tunnel was financed vary, but it seems that[2] the works were initially carried out at the risk of the Sardinian Government, the Victor Emmanuel Company meeting half the cost (estimated at £800,000 to each party) and to be given the tunnel when complete. In 1860 however when Savoy became part of France, the line of the tunnel crossed the new frontier. The French government agreed to meet half the estimated cost of the tunnel if it were completed in less than 25 years, with a substantial premium added for each year by which that period might be shortened - a premium which it probably did not expect to be called upon to pay. The works remained in Italian hands.

Cession of Savoy to France meant also that the Victor Emmanuel Railway found itself operating in two separate countries. The line in Savoy was successfully extended for eight miles towards the tunnel, as far as St Michel de Maurienne, in 1862, but about this time all the Victor Emmanuel system in Savoy was transferred to the Paris, Lyons & Mediterranean Railway. This was in no way a good thing for development of the Mont Cenis route, whether by tunnel or Fell railway: the PLM was happily carrying traffic for Italy and points east via Marseilles, 537 miles from Paris, for onward transit by sea, and had no interest in diverting it to a route which would mean a substantially shorter journey over its metals, St Michel being only 421 miles from Paris.

On the Italian side, the Victor Emmanuel line was transferred to the Piedmont State Railway; then in 1865 this in turn became one of the constituents of the *Società delle Ferrovie d'Alta Italia*: the Upper Italy Railways. The railway system of Italy was expanding rapidly: from 1862 the new Italian government encouraged railway construction as an aid to unification. A line which will shortly prove of particular interest here is the *SF Meridionale* or South Italian Railway. This extended rail communication from the *Alta Italia* at Bologna right down the East coast of Italy to Brindisi. Brassey, in partnership with Buddicom and Parent (a Belgian contractor), was responsible for construction of some 160 miles of it, and it was open through to Brindisi by 1865. Contemporaneously, the Italian government arranged for a service of mail steamers between Brindisi and Alexandria, Egypt.

The *Meridionale* was, however, of much greater importance to Britain than merely employment of British contractors. At this period trade between Britain and the Far East was increasing rapidly; in 1867 Sir Cusack Roney wrote[3] that its value, both imports and exports, amounted to one quarter of the total trade of the country. It had increased three-fold over five years, and twenty-fold over the previous fifty years. This increase, coupled with the build-up of the military in India since the mutiny of 1857, resulted in a similar increase in demand for quick postal communication with the Far East. Since 1839, the fast mails had been carried overland to

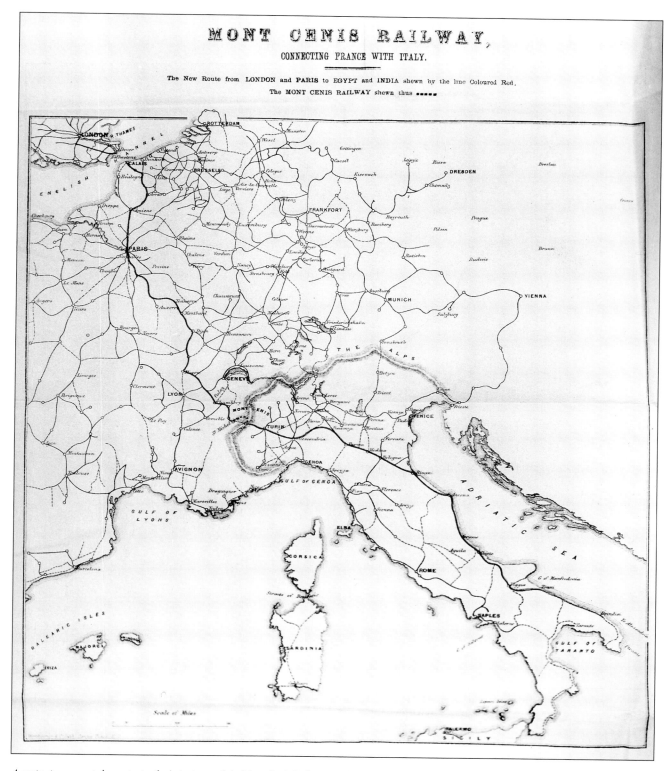

### MONT CENIS RAILWAY,
#### CONNECTING FRANCE WITH ITALY.

The New Route from LONDON and PARIS to EGYPT and INDIA shewn by the line Coloured Red.

The MONT CENIS RAILWAY shewn thus ▪▪▪▪

*A contemporary map demonstrates the importance of the Mont Cenis Railway as a link in international communications.*
**Carte d'époque montrant l'importance du Chemin de Fer du Mont Cenis en tant que lien pour les communications internationales.**
STAFFORDSHIRE RECORD OFFICE.

Marseilles, thence by steamship to Alexandria, across the Suez peninsula by land, and onward by steamship to India and China. In 1858 a postal service using the same route commenced between Britain and Australia. By the early 1860s the land journeys had been greatly accelerated by completion of railways between Calais and Marseilles, and between Alexandria and Suez (the latter was to serve until opening of the Suez Canal in 1869). Completion of the railway to Brindisi, and replacement of Marseilles by Brindisi as the port of embarkation for Alexandria, would it was clear produce a further substantial reduction in the journey time, estimated at about 36 hours. In other words, mails - and passengers - from the Far East would arrive in London a day and a half earlier.

Once the *Meridionale* was opened, the 1,400 miles of railway between Calais and Brindisi would be complete but for one break: the 48 miles of road over the Mont Cenis pass. The diligences plied between the railheads at St Michel and Susa, and were allowed 9 hours in summer and 10½ in winter; their average speed, in summer, of 5.3 mph was terribly slow compared with the speeds of train travel to which people were already accustomed, but it does seem to have been fairly reliable. In winter it was a different matter. When the snow covered the road, the diligences were replaced by sledges; their passenger accommodation was enclosed and heated, to be sure, and on hard-packed snow they ran well enough; but changes in the weather came rapidly, blizzards enveloped the col, sledge-horses floundered in deep soft snow, avalanches descended on the road and deep drifts could be encountered at any minute. The journey time expanded to 16 or 17 hours; sometimes onward progress became impossible and travellers were said to be delayed for as much as 20 or 30 hours. Nevertheless, in 1864 some 48,000 travellers and 30,000 tons of goods crossed over the pass.

Sometime during the 1850s, the thought had arisen that the diligences could be improved upon, and the large number of horses and mules required to pull them uphill

reduced, by constructing a horse tramway along the road. This was in itself fairly advanced thinking. Although the street railway with horsedrawn tramcars for passengers had originated in New York in 1832, it became popular in the USA only in the early 1850s and spread to Europe in 1855 with the opening for regular service of the first street tramway in Paris. This may, however, explain why the eventual Mont Cenis Railway, running along the road, was known in Savoy as the *chemin de fer américain*[4].

In any event all this background must have been familiar to J. B. Fell, and to Thomas Brassey too. (Indeed the value of accelerating the Eastern Mails must have impressed itself upon Brassey personally at this period, for in 1862 he contracted for 64 miles of railway in Mauritius, and in 1863 for 78 miles in Queensland.) In Fell's own account of the origin and development of the Mont Cenis Railway, given to the British Association in 1866[5], he stated that it was about four years earlier, that is in 1862, when the Italian government gave concessions for the railway to Brindisi and the great tunnel connecting France with Italy required many years for its completion, that he 'was asked to furnish a plan by which this apparently insurmountable obstacle could be overcome at an earlier period'. What he proposed 'in conjunction with Mr Brassey and some other gentlemen' was 'to construct a railway on the existing imperial road...from St. Michel...to Susa...and so put into early communication the existing lines of the two countries, and complete the new route to the East...'.

He continued: 'The two Governments' i.e., France and Italy, 'accepted the proposal on condition of their being satisfied as to the practicability of working locomotives on gradients as steep as those of the public road, combined with sharp curves, and at such an elevation as the summit of this Alpine pass'.

The maximum gradient would be 1 in 12, the minimum curve 2 chains. This meant that the locomotives must be not only powerful, but also small, with a short wheelbase. Although engineers had grappled with the problem of designing a locomotive which would be large and powerful and yet with a wheelbase flexible enough to traverse sharp curves, none had yet been conspicuously successful. Robert Fairlie, for instance, would take out his first patent for a double-bogie locomotive only in 1864. Fell, in order to increase the adhesion of small locomotives beyond that provided by their weight, considered rack-and-pinion, and grooved wheels; the system he adopted was the central rail 'on which adhesion could be obtained by the pressure of horizontal wheels worked by the engine in conjunction with, or independently of, the ordinary driving wheels'.

Fell did not invent the centre rail system, although he may have thought of it independently of earlier inventors. What he told the British Association in 1866 was: 'The use of the centre rail system appears to have been first thought of by Messrs Vignoles and Ericsson in the year 1830...In ignorance of what had been designed by those gentlemen more than thirty years ago, the Baron Seguier, in France, the writer and others in England and elsewhere, consider themselves also to be inventors of the centre rail system'.

John Ericsson is remembered as one of the

builders of Rainhill Trials competitor *Novelty*, and Charles Blacker Vignoles helped to finance that locomotive. In 1830 they took out patent no. 5995: a horizontal wheel, driven through bevel gears, was to be brought into contact with a central rail when a roller was pressed against the other side of the rail by a lever. At this date Vignoles was building a branch of the North Union Railway with a gradient of 1 in 30 and it was for this that the scheme was intended. But although experiments were carried out and models to illustrate the principle were exhibited[6], the scheme was not put fully into practice.

In 1840 Henry Pinkus managed to include horizontal driving wheels, placed either side of a central rail to assist the adhesion of a locomotive on an inclined plane, in a portmanteau patent (no. 8663) for improvements in road construction. There was no apparent outcome. In 1843, in France, Baron Séguier proposed use of a centre rail, not to increase adhesion, but as a means of preventing derailments on lines where speeds were high. He took out a patent to this effect in 1846 but again without practical outcome.

George Escol Sellers of Cincinatti however did make seven locomotives for additional

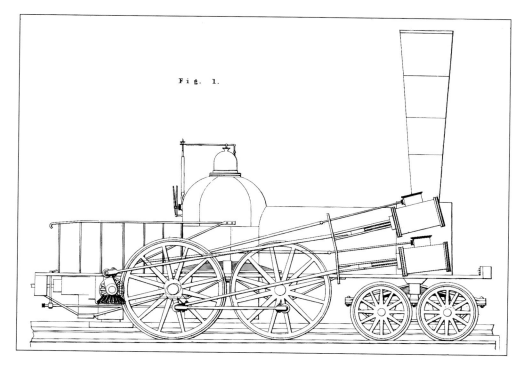

Fig. 1.

*G. E. Sellers's central rail locomotive of the 1840s had additional horizontal wheels to the rear of the driving wheels.*
**La locomotive à rail central de G. E. Sellers des années 1840 avait des roues horizontales supplémentaires à l'arrière des roues motrices.**

centre rail adhesion between 1847 and 1856[7]. His layout, as indicated in British patent no. 11793 taken out on his behalf by A. V. Newton in 1847, was for a typical American 4-4-0 of the period with an additional pair of cylinders driving, through bevel gears, a pair of horizontal wheels to the rear of the driving wheels. Five of the locomotives were made for the Panama Railroad, but this line when constructed was found to need no gradient steeper than 1 in 88 and the complications of a centre rail proved unnecessary. The other two were built for the Coal Run Railway in Pennsylvania which had inclines of 1 in 27; but the owning coal company went bankrupt before the locomotives had been fully tried out.

Whatever the priorities of centre rail traction, J. B. Fell was responsible for its adoption over Mont Cenis, and he deserves the credit for its being brought into everyday commercial use. It is fitting that the system bears his name.

British patents, in those days, gave the patentee a 14-year monopoly. During 1863-4 Fell took out first one and then a second patent covering centre rail traction. During the same period, the first Fell locomotive was designed, built and tested; from study of the patents it is clear the two processes were interlinked.

The provisional specification of his first patent, no. 227, *Improvements in Working Railway Engines and Carriages on Steep Inclines* was filed 26 January 1863. It described the nature of the invention, and it is clear that Fell's ideas of what he expected to achieve were already fully formed: added adhesion going up gradient, added braking power coming down, and security against derailments. The complete specification including drawings was filed on 24 July and in it Fell specifically does not claim originality in use of a central rail for the purposes just mentioned. What he does claim is, in two forms, the arrangement and mode of working of horizontal adhesion wheels in combination with a central rail, plus means for transmitting power to several further sets of wheels beneath the vehicles of the train

rather than the locomotive.

The first arrangement is shown only in two generalised drawings. There are four cylinders in line across the locomotive, that is two outside for the vertical wheels and two inside for the horizontal. The ends of horizontal leaf springs bear in some unspecified manner upon the crank axles of the horizontal wheels; these springs can be drawn together to press the wheels against the centre rail. The second arrangement is shown in much more detailed form, requiring eight further drawings. The cylinders for the horizontal wheels are now positioned fore-and-aft along the centre line of the locomotive. The horizontal wheels are placed under pressure by volute springs which bear against their axleboxes, and the specific means by which the load on these can be varied is shown. So too are the linkages to which these axleboxes are connected, and which maintain the crankshafts vertical when they are moved towards or away from the centre rail.

These arrangements are very close indeed to those of the first locomotive as built, and seem likely to have emerged during the spring of 1863 while it was being designed. The detail design work of this locomotive was the responsibility of A. Alexander of Brassey Jackson Betts & Co.'s Canada Works at Birkenhead, for it was there that the locomotive was built. These works had been established ten years earlier as an adjunct to Brassey's main contracting business, and had since built about 150 locomotives; few if any can have been as small and complex as the Fell locomotive.

Its gauge, and that of the eventual Mont Cenis Railway, was 1.10 metres (3 feet $7^5/_{16}$ inches). Despite all that was written at the time about the railway, I have been unable to ascertain how this precise gauge was established. Clearly, for a railway that was to occupy a narrow strip along one side of the Mont Cenis Road, and follow so far as possible its bends, narrow trains and a narrow gauge were necessary. But at this period use of narrow gauges for public railways was still rare, although locomotives on gauges as narrow as 2 feet 8 inches were in use in industry. On public railways, the 3 feet 6 inches gauge had come into use in Norway in the summer of 1861; the first locomotives for the Festiniog Railway, of about 1 foot 11¾ inches gauge, were put into service only in October 1863. There was, however, one earlier steam railway of 1.10 m gauge on the Continent: the Antwerp-Ghent line which had been operating since as early as 1844. The

same gauge was used by the Paris-Orléans Railway for its mineral branch from Mondalazac to Salle-la-Source built in 1861: horses at first hauled the trains, but locomotives were introduced in 1864.

Externally at first sight the locomotive appeared as a neat little 0-4-0ST. At Fell's request, the cylinders for and the drive to the two sets of wheels had been kept quite

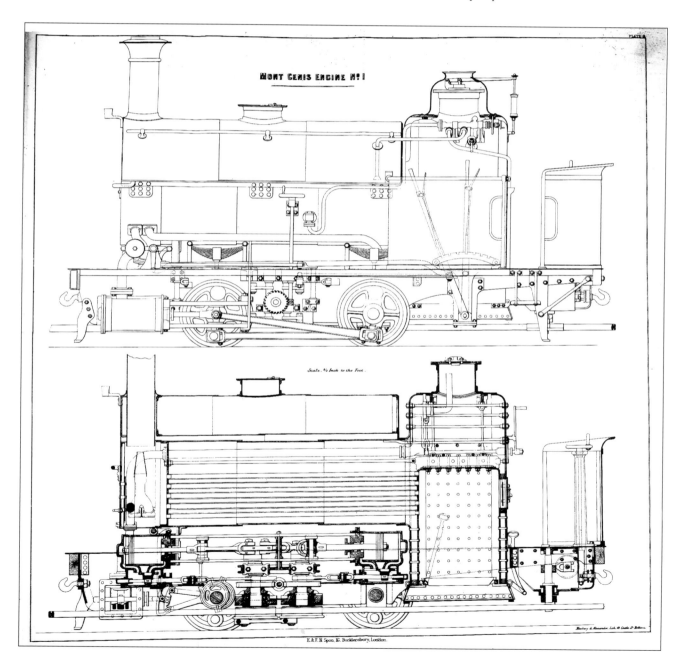

separate, so that each might be observed independently. Two outside cylinders drove the driving wheels, which also were outside the frames; everything else was squeezed in between. The valve gear for these cylinders was driven from the front axle; the space between the driving-wheel axles was taken up by the two pairs of horizontal wheels and their crank shafts. Tucked in above the driving wheel axles and below the boiler were the cylinders, motion and valve gear for the horizontal wheels.

As built the locomotive's horizontal wheels probably had flanges which fitted below the central rail - the patent drawings show this feature also. These seem to have been removed later, possibly as a result of experience that, when a poor length of track was encountered, their tendency was not to hold the locomotive down, but to lift the central rail up.

J. B. Fell was in touch with the London & North Western Railway as early as November 1862 seeking permission to experiment on one of the inclines of the Cromford & High Peak Railway; this had been leased by the LNWR the previous year. Work commenced in August 1863 on relaying one of the tracks of Whaley incline (at Whaley Bridge) to 1.10 m gauge and installing the central rail. At this date the stationary engine that had worked the incline was out of use because of subsidence, and the incline was being worked by horses. The CHP had been connected to the Stockport, Disley & Whaley Bridge Railway since 1857, the connection being above Whaley incline; at the terminus below the incline it connected with the Peak Forest Canal. Since the SD & WB was a satellite of the London & North Western Railway, and the canal was owned by the rival Manchester Sheffield & Lincolnshire Railway, one may surmise that traffic over the incline was minimal (although the incline was fully reinstated after the Fell trials).

Perhaps because it seems inherently improbable that the gauge of one track of an operating inclined plane should be altered for trials lasting several months, their actual location on the CHPR has been a matter of

controversy and many people have been led astray, including the present author when writing *Narrow Gauge Steam*. I am particularly grateful therefore to Keith Pearson for drawing my attention to T. M. A. Desbrière's 1865 paper *Études sur la Locomotion au Moyen du Rail Central* in which their location at Whaley Bridge is recorded beyond doubt, for Desbrière was present.

This trial line as built comprised, firstly, 180 yards of straight track on a gradient of 1 in $13\frac{1}{2}$ up the incline. Beyond the incline head came a level or near-level section; the trial line diverged from the CHP to reach a hillock where Fell laid a further 150 yards of track in the form of four continuous reverse curves of $2\frac{1}{2}$ chains radius, on an average gradient of 1 in 12, but with the steepest section 1 in 10. The total length of line was 800 yards. The central rail was double-headed rail laid on its side, centrally between the running rails and $7\frac{1}{2}$ inches above them.

The locomotive arrived in time for the first trials in September. At this stage it was probably named *Alpine*; later it became Mont Cenis Railway no. 1. The trials continued until the following February; they will be described shortly, but in the meantime Fell was working on another patent which must first be considered.

This patent is no. 3182 *Improvements in Railway Engines, Carriages, and Permanent Way for Steep Inclines*; it principally reflects developing ideas on the layout of Fell locomotives. The provisional specification was dated 16 December 1863. It is more detailed than the earlier one and the 'invention' is divided into nine parts not all of which were to be of lasting interest. The first part, referring back to the four-cylinders-in-line arrangement of the previous patent, described a means to couple the horizontal wheels on either side of the centre rail. In a drawing attached to the complete specification, which was filed on 15 June 1864, this is shown applied to a locomotive of the same general outline as the one already built. The specification also incorporates detailed arrangements for improving the mounting of the horizontal wheels so that 'they can give way to any

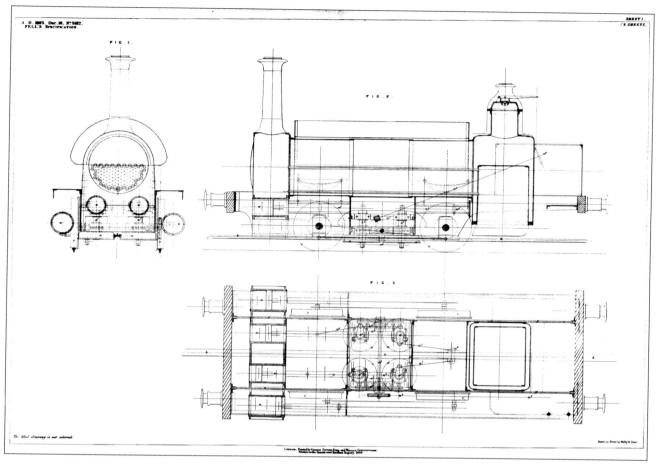

irregularities in the position of the middle rail...[but]...will bite upon the middle rail with an unvarying pressure'. It sounds like the voice of experience gained during the trials.

Another part covers driving both the horizontal and the vertical wheels from a single pair of cylinders through various arrangements of linkages and rocking shafts or crankshafts. This resulted in arrangements much less cramped, though more complicated in their geometry, than the four-cylinder arrangements; the next locomotive to be built, which will be described shortly, was of this type.

Two further parts covered fittings which were applied to the first locomotive. One of these was sledge brakes, in a pair to clasp the central rail. (Originally Fell seems to have thought in terms of ordinary brakes applied to the horizontal wheels.) These brakes became a regular feature of Fell stock. The other fitting

comprised steam jets to direct sand between the horizontal wheels and the central rail, to which condensation made it adhere; these arrangements anticipated normal steam sanding gear by more than twenty years.

Also covered in this patent were, for the centre rail, various types of rail and supports.

The principal object of the Whaley Bridge trials was, according to Fell[8], 'to prove the practicability of obtaining effective adhesion by the pressure of horizontal wheels on the centre rails, and of testing the facilities afforded by them for passing round sharp curves'. In pursuit of the latter object, two pairs of horizontal wheels were provided beneath each of the wagons - there were four of them - to minimise the extent to which the flanges of their carrying-wheels would bear against the outer rail on curves.

Early trials were no doubt private experiments, but by January 1864 Fell was evidently ready for public demonstrations: *The Times* on 9 January reported that trials of the locomotive would be made 'between 2 and 5 pm on the 12th, 13th and 14th inst.' Desbrière attended a trial on 23 January. The locomotive was halted at the foot of Whaley incline, then mounted it easily hauling the four wagons, each weighing 7 tons, despite greasy rails. At the foot of the 1 in 12 gradient, the wagons were detached and the locomotive set off light, using only the normal drive. It went only a few yards before lack of adhesion brought it to a stand. The wheels gripping the centre rail were then started, and the locomotive climbed the gradient with the greatest ease. This was repeated several times, first light engine, and then with a steadily increased number of wagons until all four were in tow. The train was easily stopped by brakes in mid-gradient (wagons as well as locomotive were braked) and on the descent, wagons leading, their horizontal wheels guided them round curves. It sounds a practised performance, and from these and similar trials the practicabilty of the centre rail system was considered proved.

The next stage was to form a company to obtain, from the French and Italian governments, concessions for the railway, as a preliminary to forming a further company to finance, build and operate it. Financially, for such activities, the times seemed promising. In the mid-1850s the popularity of railway construction as a medium for investment had at last begun to recover from the bursting of the Railway Mania bubble a decade earlier, and the early 1860s saw a mini-Railway Mania of their own.

Recovery had been aided increasingly by contractors who themselves promoted and invested in the railways they were to build. The Direct Portsmouth Railway between Godalming and Havant had been built thus by Brassey between 1853 and 1858; such 'contractors' lines' although unpopular with existing railways were valuable in filling gaps in the system. The London, Chatham & Dover, under construction at this period, was largely financed through the medium of its principal contractors, Samuel Morton Peto

and Edward Betts.

Yet with the railway map of Britain filling up, British investors' eyes were turning increasingly abroad. Something like one third of all British overseas investment in the 1860s is said to have been concerned with railway-building[9]. Promotion of the Mont Cenis Railway by British contractors to fill a vital gap in the railway system of the Continent is clearly well in tune with the thinking of the time. Some thirteen persons came together on 12 April 1864 to form the Mont Cenis Railway Concessionary Company[10]. Its object was 'to obtain the concessions for laying and working a Railway on the Public Road over the Pass of the Mont Cenis until the time when the Tunnel is completed, the free use of the Public Road being granted for the purpose...'

The list of subscribers was:
    The Duke of Sutherland
    Thomas Brassey
    Sir Morton Peto and Mr Betts
    James Lister
    T. R. Crampton
    Alex. Brogden
    James Cross
    John B. Fell
    James Brunlees
    Joseph Jopling
    T. S. Cutbill
    C. Lowinger.

Each of these took one £1,000 share, except Brassey who took three, Fell who took two, and Peto & Betts who took one between them. Anticipated expenses included surveys and estimates, and purchase of the locomotive which had been built.

It is worth having a closer look at some of the shareholders.

George Granville William Sutherland-Leveson-Gower (1828-1892), third Duke of Sutherland, was one of the wealthiest men in Britain. His fortune was derived from the Bridgewater Canal and the Liverpool & Manchester Railway through a complex process of inheritance: during this the Dukes of Sutherland had acquired the hereditary right to appoint a director to that great

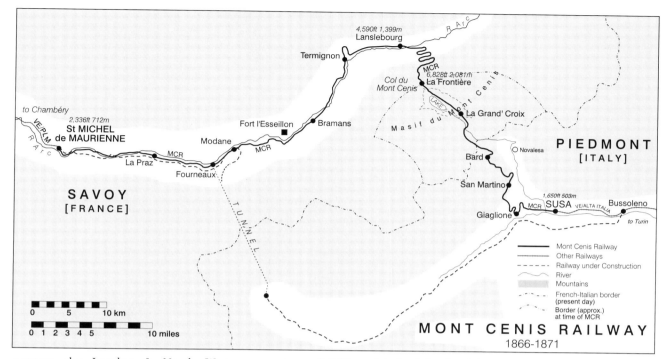

*Map of the Mont Cenis Railway.*
**Carte du Chemin de Fer du Mont Cenis**
AUTHOR.

concern the London & North Western Railway. The second duke appointed his son to that position in 1852 and he held it for the rest of his life, becoming the third duke in 1861. When young, he had come into contact with LNW Locomotive Superintendent J. E. McConnel and spent much time in Wolverton Works, which built locomotives until 1863. A clue to the duke's character may be found in a comment in his speech at the opening-day banquet in 1873 of the Isle of Man Railway (of which he had become chairman): 'I would rather be 18 hours on the footplate of an engine than make a speech at all'. One may conjecture that as an LNW director he would have become aware of the Whaley Bridge trials; their location, too, was no great distance from his seat at Trentham, Staffordshire.

Sir Morton Peto (1809-1889) had had, at this date, a contracting career as widespread and distinguished as Brassey's if not more so; it had included the vital military railway in the Crimean War, without remuneration, but his baronetcy came as a result. Much of this career had been pursued in partnership with his brother-in-law Edward Betts (1815-72); the pair had also often entered into partnerships with Brassey - for instance, for the Queensland

contract of 1863, and indeed for the Crimea railway.

Thomas Russell Crampton (1816-1888) is best remembered for his striking patent locomotives of the 1840s, in which a low centre of gravity was achieved by mounting the boiler low down with the large driving wheels to the rear of the firebox. The result was a steady-riding machine which - it is worth noting - enjoyed much greater and longer-lasting popularity in France than in England. But designing patent locomotives was but part of Crampton's long and varied career which had included laying the first successful submarine electric telegraph cable, across the English Channel in the early 1850s.

At that period too he was one of the principal promoters of the London Chatham & Dover Railway, to provide a more direct route between London and Dover than that of the South Eastern Railway. By a process of wheeling and dealing, what had at first been presented to the SER as a branch line in east Kent had become, by 1862, a competing main line from Victoria to Dover Harbour. It was Crampton who had brought Peto & Betts into the scheme both as contractors and financiers; he himself contracted for parts of the line. By

1864 attention was concentrated on completing the link across the Thames at Blackfriars to the Metropolitan Railway at Farringdon. To the Continental traffic from London this would add, it was anticipated, the Continental traffic from all the main lines from the north[11]. In this scenario support by Crampton, Peto and Betts for a vital rail link on the Continent has a clear relevance beyond any immediate financial return.

Alexander Brogden (1825-1892) had, like J. B. Fell, links with Furness - the prospectus of the eventual Mont Cenis Railway company gives 'Ulverstone' as the address of both. He was the son of John Brogden, Lancashire farmer's son turned entrepreneur whose activities included railway contracting on a large scale and, from about 1850, mining haematite iron ore in Furness. To provide a direct rail link to the South, Brogden & Sons promoted and largely built the Ulverston & Lancaster Railway. This meant crossing the estuaries of the Rivers Kent and Leven by viaducts and extensive embankments, which functioned also as land reclamation works. Alexander Brogden superintended the construction work; from about 1857 he became, in effect, senior partner in the firm as his father gradually withdrew from business (he died in 1867). Brogden probably knew as much as anyone in the Mont Cenis project about operating small steam locomotives: from 1863 the firm was buying 2 feet 10 inches gauge locomotives from Fletcher Jennings & Co. for railways of that gauge to serve its coal mines in the Ogmore valley, South Wales.

The engineer for the Ulverston & Lancaster was James Brunlees (1816-1892). To provide a northern outlet for Furness ore, Brogden and Brunlees would also be associated in constructing the Solway Junction Railway, during the same period that they were involved in the Mont Cenis. Brunlees's career is very much in the nineteenth-century tradition. He was the son of the Duke of Roxburgh's agent's gardener. He showed talent when, as a youth, he assisted surveyor Alexander Adie with surveys of roads on the Roxburgh estates, and this had led to the career of civil engineer. After a spell at Edinburgh University he worked under Adie on construction of the Bolton & Preston Railway, and was subsequently on the staff of engineers building several of the main lines in the North of England and Southern Scotland. A comparatively minor venture was to engineer the Gorseddau Tramway, a feeder line to Portmadoc Harbour, during 1855-7: 3 feet gauge, 8 miles long, operated by horse and gravity.

Part of a much greater undertaking was Brunlees's decision to use cable haulage with stationary engines on the 5 feet 3 inches gauge São Paulo Railway, Brazil, for which he became engineer in 1856. Surmounting a 2,650-feet escarpment required four inclined planes with a gradient of 1 in 9.75. These were suggested to Brunlees by his assistant D. M. Fox, whom he had despatched to Brazil to make the surveys and, eventually, superintend construction. The line would be completed only in 1867: construction was still in progress when, early in 1864, Brunlees accompanied J. B. Fell in making a careful examination of the line of the proposed Mont Cenis Railway.

Like Brunlees, James Cross (1829-1894) had trained under Alexander Adie. He had subsequently become engineer to the St Helens Canal & Railway Co. and, when the St Helens Railway was acquired by the LNWR in 1864, he leased its works and set up as a locomotive builder. He evidently had an inclination towards locomotives which incorporated technological advance: he had already, in 1863, built the 2-4-2T *White Raven* for W. Bridges Adams to try out his newly-invented radial axleboxes, and in 1864 he would, as we shall shortly see, build Mont Cenis Railway no. 2.

Joseph Jopling was the elder brother of C. M. Jopling who had been Fell's partner on the Central Italian Railway but who had died from malaria in 1863. He too worked for Brassey but seems to have had little subsequent involvement with the Mont Cenis Railway. T. S. Cutbill, of 13 Gresham Street, London EC, was appointed secretary to the company; he was associated with Brassey in other ventures such as the Mauritius Railway.

J. B. Fell approached the French and

Italian governments, on behalf of the company, for concessions for the proposed temporary railway. No financial assistance was requested: it was anticipated that, in its period of operation until the tunnel line was opened, it would produce a profit after reimbursing capital and interest.

The French government, however, required to be further convinced of the practicability of the scheme before granting a concession; the Italian government promised a concession once the French granted one. To meet the French requirement a second trial line was constructed, this time along part of what would become the most severe section of the eventual railway, the zig-zag ascent from Lanslebourg to the summit. This line was $1^1/_4$ miles long with a ruling gradient of 1 in 12 and an average of 1 in 13, laid out along the outer side of the road except where, to turn one of the hairpin bends (the third from the bottom) it went into an omega-loop of about 2 chains radius. It commenced at an altitude of 5,321 feet above sea level, and ascended to 5,815 feet: the effect on operation of the severe climate at such an altitude was one of the points at issue. Rails were borrowed from the Victor Emmanuel Railway, the running rails and the centre rail being double-headed rail of 75 lb/yd.

The trial line had been laid before 23 January 1865, for on that date J. B. Fell mentioned it in a letter to the Postmaster General, Lord Stanley of Alderley, in which he appraised him officially of the advantages of the proposed undertaking for carriage of the Indian Mails.

Meanwhile the second locomotive was being built by James Cross at St Helens, the first to be built by his newly-established business, though its builder's number was 2 (*White Raven* presumably being considered no. 1). Its MCR running number also became 2. Brassey's works was very busy at this period, which may be a reason why the order went to Cross. It is illustrated on page 26.

Like no. 1, no. 2 was designed by Alexander after consultation with Fell; its layout was one of several covered by Fell's second patent (3182 of 1863). There were two inside cylinders, beneath the smokebox. Piston rods projecting in the usual way from the rear of the cylinders were connected by rods to the horizontal driving wheels - two pairs, coupled by rods longitudinally and, across the locomotive, by gears to maintain the effect of quartering. This coupling across the locomotive was an early modification, made when it was found that the locomotive would not work without it. The vertical wheels were driven by piston rods which projected from the front of the cylinders, terminating in crossheads working between slidebars. In each crosshead was a vertical slot, through which passed a horizontal pin attached to the upper part of a vertical rocking lever mounted on one of a pair of in-line transverse shafts. At the outer ends of each of these shafts was attached a further rocking lever. From this a rod, described by Fell as a 'transmitting rod', led back to a bar which reciprocated in guides and which was in turn attached by a connecting rod to one of the rear driving wheels. These were coupled in the usual way to the front pair. All wheels, vertical and horizontal, were of the same diameter and the layout enabled the connecting rods to all wheels to be of the same length. At this period, drive via rocking levers was not so unconventional as it would later become but none the less, given the stage which engineering techniques had reached, design and construction of this locomotive must have stretched those concerned.

The locomotive had side tanks. A curious feature, repeated on later Mont Cenis locomotives, was lack of access to the footplate from the sides of the locomotive, but only from the rear: perhaps a safety feature on a line which was to be located, in so many places, along the edge of a precipice.

The Lanslebourg trials attracted official observers not only from the French government but also from the governments of Italy, Britain, Austria and Russia. The British government sent that noted Inspecting Officer of Railways Capt. Henry Whatley Tyler, Royal Engineers (1827-1908). Tyler had recently drawn attention to the potential for railways of narrow gauge as exemplified by the

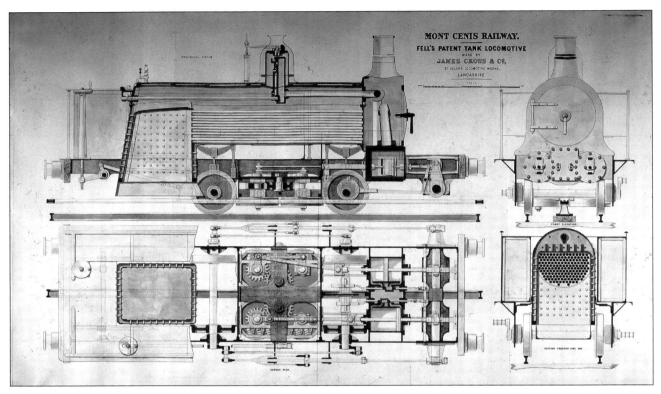

*The second Fell locomotive was built in 1864-5 by James Cross for the Lanslebourg trials. Unlike the first, it had only two cylinders; drive to the horizontal wheels was direct, but drive to the vertical wheels was via rocking levers and inclined rods.*

**La deuxième locomotive Fell fut construite en 1864-5 par James Cross pour les essais de Lanslebourg. Contrairement à la première, elle n'avait que 2 cylindres; le mécanisme moteur des roues horizontales état directe, mais le mécanisme moteur des roues verticales se faisait par des leviers à bascule et des bielles inclinées.**

FLINTSHIRE RECORD OFFICE.

introduction of steam locomotives on the Festiniog Railway; he would later become a protagonist of the Westinghouse brake. He was a man whose approach was as human as it was forthright.

The French Imperial Commission had as its president M. Conte, *Ingénieur en chef des Ponts et Chaussées de France*, accompanied by MM. Bochet, Guinard and Perrin. For this commission trials commenced on 28 February 1865; they attracted 600 spectators. The weather was satisfactorily wintry: on 4 March after three days and nights of snow it was so cold that that despite fires in the locomotive shed the water was frozen in the cylinders of the locomotive and the oil in its journals. Nevertheless steam was raised and the locomotive - no. 1, the only one yet available - ran well all day, round the sharpest curves, and stopping and starting in the most difficult places[12]. Indeed it was eventually noted that adhesion was better in winter than summer for snow, when removed from the rails, left them dry but in summer road dust mixed with damp to render them greasy.

Captain Tyler came during the spring. He reported the presence of not only locomotive no. 1 and four wagons, but also no. 2 locomotive and a passenger carriage - a short-wheelbase four-wheeler, in which twelve passengers sat facing one another, six a side. Of no. 2, however, he found that 'unfortunately some of the parts in front of the cylinder connected with the vertical wheels required strengthening, and it was not desirable...to test the engine much...until the new parts...had been received from England.'

However he was able to run it, with a load of 16 tons in three wagons, for over a mile at an average speed of 10 mph. This was quicker than the average speed of no. 1 on similar trials. Nevertheless, he did note that no. 1, despite inability to generate sufficient steam continuously for a long run such as the proposed MCR, and an unfortunate tendency to drip oil from the motion over the horizontal wheels, had satisfactorily run over 100 miles hauling materials and ballast for the experimental line.

It was proposed to carry the Mont Cenis

traffic by three trains each way daily - a mail train which would carry the mails, first and second class passengers and their luggage in 4 to 4½ hours from end to end; a mixed train carrying passengers of all three classes, luggage, parcels and freight in 6 to 6½ hours, and a goods train in 8 hours.

Trials were increasingly arranged to demonstrate that these trains, particularly the first, were practicable. On 19 July no. 2 made five runs: three runs hauling four wagons and the coach, all the stock available, weighing 24 tons, followed by two more with three wagons, weighing 16 tons and representing the mail train. Steam pressure was consistently higher at the end of the run than at the start. The first three runs were made in 9, 11 and 10 minutes respectively; the last two were both made in 7½ minutes. To meet the promised schedule, the mail train would have to maintain 14 kph (8.70 mph) up gradients of 1 in 14, and 12 kph (7.46 mph) up gradients of 1 in 12[13]. That meant that it would have to run a distance of 2 km (1¼ miles) of 1 in 14 in 8.57 minutes, or 1 in 12 in 10 minutes - demonstrably within its capability.

It was on this occasion that Frederick Hardman, special correspondent of *The Times* based in Florence, was shown over the experimental line personally by Fell. His report was published on 29 July and was one of many, well-informed and sympathetic, that he was to provide about the Mont Cenis Railway: their publication may perhaps have been aided by frequent presence of the editor, John Thadeus Delane, as a guest of the Duke of Sutherland at his Scottish seat, Dunrobin Castle[14].

The trials on 19 July were also the occasion of the last of six visits made by the French commissioners. In their eventual report their principal conclusions were that the proposed system of traction, with engines of the type which worked the last trials, was applicable to Mont Cenis, and that there was no danger to public safety for the central rail provided a guarantee against derailments and a means to brake trains.

Meanwhile, there had been three days of similar trials for the Italian commissioners (Signor Negretti, president) and the Russians - the Austrians had been in the spring - and, on 31 July, a day of trials for James Brunlees himself. This concluded the official series, although there were more trials, including brake tests, before Brassey, Buddicom and Blount on 29 and 30 November.

James Brunlees, reporting in August 1865 to the concessionary company on the results of the trials, stated that throughout them no. 2 with a 16-ton load maintained a speed of nearly 10 mph where 7½ mph was required, and with a 24-ton load, 6 to 8 mph where 4¼

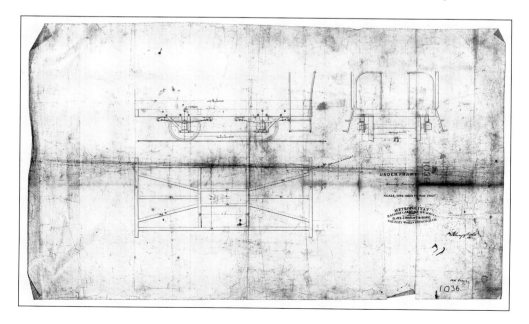

*Metropolitan Railway Carriage & Wagon Co. drawing no. 1036 of 9 February 1865 depicts the underframe of a tramway carriage for Mr Fell: presumably the carriage used at the Lanslebourg trials.*
**Dessin no. 1036 par Metropolitan Carriage & Wagon Co. datant du 9 février 1865, montrant le châssis d'un wagon de tramway pour Mr Fell: sans doute le wagon fut utilisé lors des essais de Lanslebourg.**

THE MONT CENIS FELL RAILWAY

mph was required. The principle, he considered, for ascending a steep and tortuous mountain pass was established beyond a doubt. An element of euphoria appeared: here was a locomotive able to go anywhere a horse could go - the implications were clear, not just for Mont Cenis, but for all mountain passes.

The French concession was eventually made on 4 November 1865 when the Emperor Napoleon III, who had marched his troops over Mont Cenis in 1859 and took a personal interest in the railway, made an Imperial Decree to authorise construction and working of a locomotive line along the *Route Impériale* number 6, between St Michel and the frontier. The Italian concession followed on 17 December. Both concessions were to last only until the tunnel opened to regular through traffic.

So what had been happening in the tunnel workings? When work had commenced, it was forecast to take seven years - that is, to be completed in 1864. That, clearly, was wildly out. But the same slow progress, which had prompted Fell and his associates to develop a means to take a railway over the top, had equally prompted the tunnel engineers to develop accelerated methods of tunnelling. What Fell was doing for central rail traction, the Savoyard engineer Germain Sommeiller did for drilling machinery powered by compressed air - that is, although he did not invent it, he brought it first into practical use, with the assistance of others, notably Severino

Grattoni who was in charge of the tunnel workings and Sébastien Grandis, chief engineer of the Sardinian Railways. Their first compressed-air drills replaced hand drills, for boring the holes for the explosive charges, in the Italian end of the tunnel in the summer of 1861; and they were subsequently improved. Water wheels provided the compressed air; once used, it benefited the tunnel's ventilation. Compressed-air drilling machinery was introduced at the French end in 1863.

The consequence was that whereas tunnellers starting from the Italian entrance had been able to bore only 725 metres by the end of 1860, by the end of 1865 they had bored 3,087.5 metres. Likewise those starting at the French entrance had achieved only 921 metres by the end of 1862, but had increased this to 2,222.05 metres by the end of 1865.

But the techniques were still new, and nature of the rock to be found in the centre of the tunnel still uncertain. Estimates of the time needed to complete the tunnel could be no more than informed guesses. Captain Tyler visited the workings and put it at least seven to eight years in his report of June 1865, observing also that approach railways through difficult country had still to be built. Brunlees, noting that tunnellers at the French end had recently passed from schist into exceptionally hard quartz, put it at ten to twelve years. The promoters of the Mont Cenis Railway went ahead with their scheme.

# CHAPTER THREE
# FORMING THE COMPANY
# & BUILDING THE LINE

With the onset of winter, the long interval between completion of the Lanslebourg trials and the grants of concessions had deprived the railway promoters of the chance to commence construction during the autumn of 1865. It was also to have severe financial repercussions.

Fell, who seems to have dealt personally with flotation of the company, wrote to the Duke of Sutherland on 11 January 1866 enclosing a revised draft prospectus for corrections. On 22 January *The Times* reported that 'A company is being formed...' to build a railway over Mont Cenis, adding financial and other information in such detail that it can only have come from the promoters themselves. On 1 February Fell sent the duke a copy of the 'definite prospectus', informing him that it was proposed 'to take advantage of the first favourable day' for bringing the Mont Cenis company 'before the public'.

They could scarcely have chosen a worse moment. The concessionary company had been formed at a time of optimism, and railway share prices had continued, with fluctuations, to rise until November 1865. But that was to prove the peak, and the rise had been fuelled by increasingly doubtful financial practices: at the commencement of a railway contract, a contractor would agree to accept payment in shares of the company concerned, upon which there could be no return before the railway was opened. But he would use these shares as security to borrow from finance houses the funds he needed to finance construction. There were, of course, innumerable ramifications, but in effect this was a card house, and it needed only one card to be removed from the base for the whole edifice to tumble. It had been trembling during the latter part of 1865, when the finance houses at last became reluctant to provide; in January 1866 Watson & Overend,

contractors, failed with liabilities of £1¹/₂ million and the noted railway promoter Thomas Savin who had been financing them went bankrupt on 5 February.

The Mont Cenis promoters, however, took the plunge. The company was incorporated on 7 February, and on 10 February *The Times* reported that its prospectus had been issued.

The Mont Cenis Railway Company (Limited) - to give it its full title - was incorporated as company no. 2820c under the Companies Act 1862. This had consolidated earlier legislation passed since 1855, and expanded upon it, to produce limited liability companies of the type which remain familiar today. (It is noteworthy, when studying MCR records, that with correspondence one is still in a Dickensian era of pen and ink and copperplate handwriting, produced presumably by clerks on high stools; but with printed material - memorandum and articles, prospectus, annual reports and so on - one enters a recognisably modern world.) The principal objects of the company were, predictably, to purchase 'certain concessions granted by His Imperial Majesty the Emperor of the French, and His Majesty the King of Italy' for construction of the railway, and the construction, maintenance and working of it; less predictably they included provision for operating road transport over the route or part of it. Surplus profits, after providing for debenture interest, a seven per cent dividend on shares, a bond redemption fund and a bonus fund, were to be divided half-and-half between shareholders and 'Brassey, Fell and Company, the present Concessionaires', that is, the concessionary company. On expiry of the concessions, the company was to be liquidated and proceeds again divided equally between the shareholders and Brassey, Fell and Co.

The prospectus advised intending

# MONT CENIS RAILWAY COMPANY
## (LIMITED).

SHARE CAPITAL £250,000, WITH POWER TO BORROW £125,000 ON BONDS BEARING 7 PER CENT. INTEREST.

### ISSUE OF
## SHARE CAPITAL, £250,000,

In 12,500 Shares of £20 each.    £1 payable on Application ; £3 on Allotment ;
Residue in Calls of £4 at intervals of not less than Three Months.

#### President.
THE DUKE OF SUTHERLAND, K.G.

#### Chairman.
SIR JAMES HUDSON, G.C.B.

#### Directors.

| | |
|---|---|
| THOS. BRASSEY, ESQ., 4, Great George St., S.W. | EDWARD BLOUNT, ESQ, 3, Rue de la Paix, Paris. |
| DUKE OF VALLOMBROSA, Cannes, France. | JERVOISE SMITH, ESQ., 47, Belgrave Square. |
| LORD ABINGER, Eccleston Square, S.W. | T. R. CRAMPTON, ESQ., 12, Gt. George St., S.W. |
| SIR M. PETO, BART., M.P., 9, Great George St., S.W. | W. B. BUDDICOM, ESQ., Pembedw, Flintshire. |
| SIR ROBERT DALLAS, BART., 52, Rutland Gate, S.W. | ALEX. BROGDEN, ESQ., Ulverstone. |

JOHN B. FELL, ESQ., Spark Bridge, Ulverstone.

#### Bankers.

| | |
|---|---|
| MESSRS. SMITH, PAYNE & SMITHS, 1, Lombard Street, LONDON. | MESSRS. E. BLOUNT & CO., PARIS. |
| UNION BANK, LIVERPOOL. | THE CREDIT GENEVOIS, GENEVA. |
| | MESSRS. FRENCH & CO., FLORENCE. |

#### Engineer.
JAMES BRUNLEES, ESQ.

#### Solicitors.
MESSRS. FRESHFIELDS & NEWMAN, 5, Bank Buildings, Lothbury.

#### Brokers.
MESSRS. LAURENCE, SON & PEARCE, Angel Court, Throgmorton Street, E.C.

#### Secretary.
T. S. CUTBILL, ESQ., 13, GRESHAM STREET, E.C.

## PROSPECTUS.

CONCESSIONS have been obtained from the French and Italian Governments for constructing and working a Locomotive Railway over the Mont Cenis.

This Railway crosses the Alps from St. Michel in Savoy, to Susa in Piedmont, a distance of forty-eight miles, connecting the Paris, Lyons and Mediterranean, and Victor Emmanuel Railways in France, with the Lombard-Venetian, Central and Southern Railways of Italy, thus completing the last link of a direct line of 1,406 miles from Calais to the Port of Brindisi on the Adriatic, whereby an improved route will be created from France and England to Italy, Egypt, and the East, and an important saving of time effected in the transit of the Indian Mail as reported by Captain Tyler, R.E., to the Board of Trade.

The Mont Cenis Railway will be constructed on the existing Imperial road, the grant of a sufficient width of which, free of charge, has been made by the two Governments, and the width so appropriated will be fenced off from the remaining portion of the road. This may be considered equal to a subvention of £200,000, as the works, if constructed without this privilege, would cost at least that additional sum.

For working this line, the centre rail system of Locomotives will be adopted.

The practicability of the system was first proved by trials made on the Cromford and High Peak Railway, in England, during the winter of 1863 ; and these trials, as a condition of granting the Concession, were required by the French Government to be repeated on a larger scale on one of the highest and steepest portions of the Mont Cenis, where the system has recently been submitted to every variety of test before Commissions of Engineers appointed by the French, Italian, English, Russian, and Austrian Governments.

These five Royal Commissions, in their official reports, have concurred in expressing their conviction that the trials made on the mountain have fully proved the practicability and safety of working the proposed railway over the Mont Cenis. And the complete success of the system having thus been established, the Governments of France and Italy have granted the Concessions for the railway, and the privileges asked for.

investors that the share capital was £250,000 in £20 shares, of which £1 was payable on application, £3 on allotment and the remainder in calls of £4; there was power to borrow £125,000 in 7 per cent bonds. The grant of a part of the Imperial road for use by the railway was considered equivalent to a subvention of £200,000, the saving in cost of engineering works which would otherwise have been needed.

The cost of the line based on Mr Brunlees's estimates, continued the prospectus, would not exceed £375,000, or £8,000 per mile including rolling stock and the costs of the locomotive trials already made. It was intended to open the entire line in May 1867; completion of the tunnel, 'taking the most favourable view...based upon the greatest length executed in any two years' could not take place earlier than 1874. A 'very liberal tariff' for carriage of passengers and goods had been sanctioned by the governments, the rates being those then charged by the diligences and other conveyances. Seven years of operation, plus the value of the plant at the end of that period, would produce after paying off capital and interest - a detailed table showed - a profit of £233,664. If there was a substantial increase in traffic over the pass - and experience elsewhere suggested that there would be - the profit would be much higher.

The undertaking was, in short, to be a real little gold brick. Those responsible for it were listed as:

President:    the Duke of Sutherland
Chairman:    Sir James Hudson
Directors:    Thos. Brassey; Duke of Vallombrosa; Lord Abinger; Sir M. Peto; Sir Robert Dallas; Edward Blount; Jervoise Smith; T. R. Crampton; W. B. Buddicom; Alex. Brogden; John B. Fell;
Engineer:    James Brunlees
Secretary:    T. S. Cutbill.

*Announcing formation of the MCR company, the* ILLUSTRATED LONDON NEWS *for 10 February 1866 showed readers what the ascent from Lanslebourg looked like. The train is a figment of the engraver's imagination: the trial line ran along the next two traverses above it.*
**Ce journal londonien illustré, le 'Illustrated London News' du 10 février 1866, annonçant la formation de la compagnie du CF du Mont Cenis, montrait aux lecteurs le tracé de l'ascension à partir de Lanslebourg. Le train est fictif: la ligne d'essai courait le long des deux lignes en zigzag situées au dessus.**

Most of these we have met already. Of those we have not, Sir James Hudson (1810-1885) had been British minister in Turin from 1851 until his retirement in 1863, after which he continued to live principally in Italy. An Italophile and friend of Cavour, he had been pressing for diversion of the Indian mails to the Italian route via Ancona since as early as 1861. He is said to have seen locomotive no. 1 on trial at Whaley Bridge[15] and may well have been instrumental in obtaining the goodwill of the Italian authorities towards the Mont Cenis Railway.

Lord Abinger was described by Fell to the Duke of Sutherland, in his letter of 1 February 1866, as 'Mr Brunlees' friend'. William Frederick Scarlett (1826-1892), third Baron Abinger, educated at Eton and Trinity College Cambridge, had joined the Scots Fusilier Guards in 1846 and saw action in the Crimea at Inkerman and Balaclava. This may well have provided the opportunity to observe both the value of the Crimea railway, and the efficiency with which it was built. He appears to have been a serving soldier throughout the Mont Cenis episode, but this does not seem to have prevented him from playing an active part in the railway company's affairs.

The Duke of Vallombrosa came from an old feudal family of the kingdom of Sardinia; his residence may have been a château near Dreux, west of Paris, for it was from there that he wrote to the Duke of Sutherland in September 1866, although his address as given on the prospectus was Cannes. Jervoise Smith and Sir Robert Dallas represented Smith, Payne and Smiths, bankers to the company; Jervoise Smith (1828-1884) was a partner. Fell had had earlier dealings in Furness with this firm.

T. S. Cutbill did not remain secretary for long, for by October 1866 he had given way to Walter J. C. Cutbill.

*The Times*, on the same page on which it reported issue of the prospectus, commented drily (in another item) that the position of some of the most speculative of the financial companies continued to be a matter of uncertainty, which added to the prevalence of distrust in all classes of securities. That spring was not a good time to float a company. One finance house after another failed or got into difficulties. Eventually on 11 May there was panic when the old-established house of Overend, Gurney Ltd failed, and so did Peto & Betts. The great contractor Sir Morton Peto, who had started the fund to guarantee the Great Exhibition of 1851 with a contribution of £50,000, was bankrupt, and 30,000 of his men were out of work[16]. By August the London Chatham & Dover Railway Company was unable to meet its liabilities and went into receivership. Crampton lost heavily, but survived. Brassey survived the crisis too, despite immense liabilities. His reaction was not to suspend payment, but to press his railway construction works forward as quickly as possible so that, on completion, his investment became marketable. In general, the financial crisis of 1866 depressed the economy for the next three years, and railway construction for four.

And as if the financial crisis were not enough, a House of Commons Select Committee on East India Communications, in its report printed in July, was 'not able to recommend that any steps should at present be taken' towards diverting the Indian Mail over the Mont Cenis Railway and through Italy.

By August it was clear that the Mont Cenis Railway company did not qualify for a quotation on the Stock Exchange, and to achieve this the directors were called upon to take up an additional five shares each. Writing to the Duke of Sutherland on 22 August, Lord Abinger referred to 'the default of Sir Morton Peto' and commented, of the three other directors still to take up their extra shares, 'Brunlees is abroad and Fell will pay - Crampton I fear probably will not'. Peto had disappeared from the list of directors in the report to the first general meeting of shareholders, held on 7 August.

Despite all the problems, by 21 August a total of 8,678 shares had been taken up by 448 shareholders. Brassey was the largest shareholder with 945 shares, followed by Brogden with 792. The Duke of Sutherland was third with 542. Abinger had 292 shares,

Brunlees 137, Crampton 237 and Fell himself 242. Two typical small shareholders were Sarah Binns, widow of Hoddesdon, Herts, and Jas. M. Field, clergyman of Oxendon near Northampton, with 10 shares each; there were many others - bankers, widows, doctors, a tailor and a cotton broker among them.

Much of the early part of 1866 was taken up by preparation of detailed plans and sections for approval by the French and Italian governments, and other preliminary work. Construction of the railway started, however, in March[17]. The railway was to be 79.2 km (49 miles 17 chains) long. The concessions retained 6 metres width of road for road traffic; since its total width was normally 10 metres, this left 4 metres (a little over 13 feet) for the railway. Much of the road lay along a shelf on the side of the mountain; the masonry which supported it had to be examined, strengthened and extended, and much of the roadway had to be widened. A substantial wooden fence had to be provided, between the railway and the remaining road, to keep horses, mules and cattle from straying on to the track.

At villages, the railway was to diverge from the road to follow its own right-of-way: this happened at St Michel, Modane, Bramans, Termignon, Lanslebourg and Susa. Where there were bends in the road which were too sharp for the railway's minimum radius of 40 metres (1.988 chains) it had again to diverge from the road - on some of the hairpins, the railway's minimum radius could be maintained only by tunnelling into the hillside. The road had originally left the Italian side of the summit plateau by a gradual descent down a shelf cut upon the rocky mountainside; this had been found excessively liable to avalanches, and the road had been diverted down a steep zig-zag known as *Les Echelles*, the ladders. This in turn was too severe for the railway, which re-utilised the original course of the road. However it was necessary to protect it by some 600 metres of masonry avalanche shelter: this was a reconstruction of an earlier avalanche shelter provided for road traffic.

The altitudes of the railway at the various points along its course are of such prime importance that it is frustratingly difficult to establish them with certainty - rather, consulting a dozen different sources produces as many variations in the figures. Some instances: the altitude of the summit of the line, at the Col du Mont Cenis, was quoted in *The Times* on 2 September 1867, as 6,700 feet, but *Engineering* on 26 June 1868 gave 6,870 feet, and *The Engineer* on 31 August 1866 2,125 metres (6,974 feet). Others preferred to give figures for the rise between the termini and the summit. Sir Cusack Roney in *Rambles on Railways* gives the rise from St Michel to the summit as 4,165 feet and from Susa 4,880 feet. For the same rises, Whymper, in *Scrambles amongst the Alps...*, gives 4,460 feet and 5,211 feet respectively.

At the present day, Michelin map no. 244 gives the following spot heights: St Michel, 712 metres (2,336 feet), Lanslebourg, 1,399 metres (4,590 feet), Col du Mont Cenis, 2,081 metres (6,828 feet), Susa, 503 metres (1,650 feet).

By way of comparison, the altitude of the summit of Ben Nevis, the highest point in the British Isles, is 4,406 feet. Snowdon Summit station, the highest point reached by rail, is 3,493 feet; Druimuachdar Summit, the highest point reached by a main line is 1,484 feet. *Engineering*, on 19 June 1868, considered that there were only two places where railways reached a higher altitude than the Mont Cenis: both of them in the American Rockies.

On the basis of Michelin's figures, then, the rise from St Michel to the col is 4,492 feet, and from Susa, 5,178 feet. The climb from Susa was far the more severe, for the distance was 17 miles 26 chains, compared with 31 miles 70 chains from St Michel to the col. But of the latter figure, the 25 miles 58 chains as far as Lanslebourg were generally easily graded, while from Lanslebourg to the col 682 metres (2,238 feet) had to be gained in 6 miles 12 chains.

Brunlees stated that some ten miles of the railway were above the snow line for five months of the year[18]. On the plateau snow presented little problem, for gales funnelled between the mountains blew it clear. The

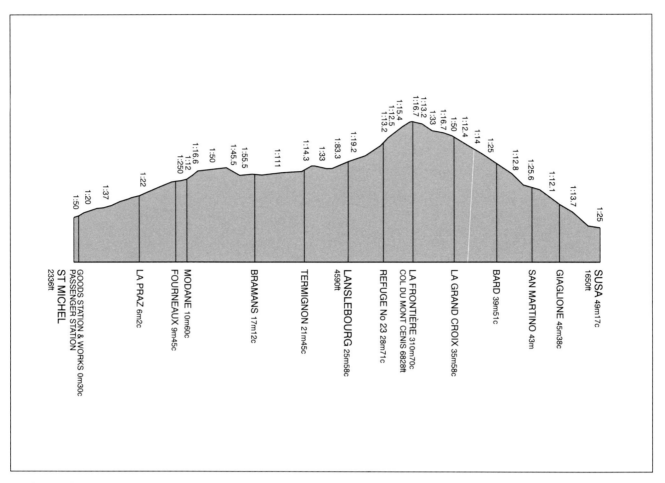

*Gradient profile of the Mont Cenis Railway.*
**Les inclinaisions du Chemin de Fer du Mont Cenis**
AUTHOR.

problem arose on the approaches, and over the col itself. Where the road was carried along a mountainside shelf, deep drifts formed year after year in the angle between the road and the mountainside. On the French side of the col, the railway was placed on the outer edge of the road: for the most part, it was anticipated, snowploughs and men with shovels would be able to tip such snow as accumulated on the track into the valley below. Only in a few places towards the top and over the col was it necessary to protect the railway by what were then called 'covered ways' which we now know as snowsheds. These were to be built from timber, roofed over with corrugated iron, and strong enough to withstand the weight of the snow and the force of the gales.

On the Italian side, the railway for most of the way was laid on the inner edge of the road beside the mountain. Why it was laid out like

this is not clear: it was subject not only to drifts, from which it was protected by snowsheds, but also to avalanches of snow and rocks. Where these were expected, the railway was covered over by the most substantial masonry avalanche shelters. However on the Italian side the climate is much milder than on the French: Roney noted vines being cultivated beside the road at an altitude of 3,795 feet, although on the French side they could not be cultivated above St Michel (2,336 feet). On such a south-facing slope the risk of avalanches is much greater than on a north-facing one, and it may be that the railway could be, on the Italian side, most easily protected against them if it were tucked in against the mountainside before being built over. This is, however, conjecture.

J. B. Fell was appointed 'the Managing Director at the Mont Cenis', according to the first report to shareholders, and the works were 'being constructed, and the material purchased, under the direct superintendence of the Company's Agents'. From this it appears that the work was being done by direct labour, although Brassey was sometimes said to be the contractor - perhaps he was so closely associated with the company that in the public mind it was not distinguished from his contracting business. On the Italian side there certainly was a contractor - indeed the contractor appointed initially was found unsatisfactory and was replaced by Gianoli & Canova, which firm was at work by September 1866.

Early in 1866, following personal communication between the Postmaster General Lord Stanley of Alderley and the President of the Board of Trade T. Milner Gibson, it was decided to send 'an Officer of Engineers' - namely, Captain Tyler - to Italy on behalf of the two departments, to inspect the whole of the proposed Italian route for the Eastern mails. He was to report on its likely time-saving, punctuality and cost. He was allowed one guinea a day personal expenses and cost of travel - an assistant was to get £1 only, plus travel - and instructed to set off on 10 April.

From Tyler's second report[19], which was submitted to the Duke of Montrose (who had succeeded Lord Stanley as PMG) on 19 July 1866, we can get an insight into initial progress with Mont Cenis Railway works. Work was in progress, on the Italian side, in six places on tunnels and embankments needed for the railway to deviate round the sharpest curves on the road, and in three more between Lanslebourg and the summit. West of Lanslebourg, viaducts and bridges were being built, as was the deviation away from the road at St Michel; work on other deviations past villages was about to start. A contract had been placed with Brogden & Co. for 3,000 tons of rails, chairs and fishplates for the Italian side; those for France were to be supplied by 'the "Terre Noire" Company of Lyons'. To minimise delays at the termini, cranes were to be provided on the platforms to transfer the mails between Mont Cenis Railway trains and

their standard gauge connections. Captain Tyler anticipated completion by 1 June 1867 or before the following winter at the latest.

Fell originally intended to have two classes of locomotive - one primarily to take heavy loads slowly up the steepest gradients between Susa and Lanslebourg, and another which, while able to work over the 1 in 12, would also be able to run at higher speeds on easily-graded sections between Lanslebourg and St Michel. The latter would have had three or four cylinders with separate drives to large vertical wheels and to smaller horizontal ones. However only one class of engine, with a single pair of cylinders, to work throughout the line was sanctioned by Fell's co-directors. As things turned out, they would have done better to heed him, for the company was to pay dearly for its initial reliance on locomotives of a single type which proved unsatisfactory.

A. Alexander was appointed Locomotive Engineer to the company, and Brassey's Canada Works quoted for construction. But the directors then belatedly discovered that French law prohibited importation of foreign machinery subject to a French patent. Fell had taken out a patent or patents in France, but one wonders also whether Baron Séguier was a problem. In any event the Mont Cenis company had to seek a French builder. This proved difficult, for those French locomotive builders with the best reputations were already fully occupied. An offer to build ten locomotives was made by Emile Gouin et Cie of Paris, who had already built two locomotives of 1.10 m gauge for the Mondalazac to Salle-la-Source line. After making a preliminary inspection of the premises, Alexander put in a highly adverse report, but it was to this firm that the order went. On 22 August 1866 Lord Abinger wrote to the Duke of Sutherland that the locomotives were all on order for delivery in February, March and April.

The locomotives were designed by Alexander, and his designs were submitted to and passed by the board of directors who included, as we have seen, several distinguished engineers. With trouble ahead, this is worth noting. To allow access to the front of the cylinders and the valve chests all

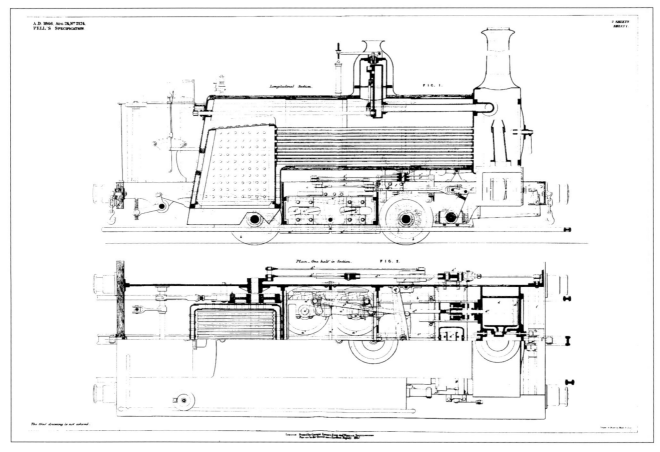

the reciprocating driving machinery was moved to the rear of the cylinders. The quartering of the horizontal driving wheels was maintained not by clattering gearwheels but by coupling them through an ingenious arrangement of cranks, rods, slides and transverse levers. Both layouts were among several covered by a third patent which Fell took out, no. 2174 of 1866. The provisional specification is dated 24 August, but the patent was sealed, with detailed drawings, only on 19 February 1867. Evidently, ideas on the best layout were continuing to evolve after the order had been placed.

The valve gear was Stephenson's link motion, driven from the front axle and outside the frames. Because of the instability of four-wheeled tank engines with a lot of overhang, the locomotives were designed as 0-4-2Ts, the trailing wheels being allowed what Fell described as 'a lateral movement'[20]. There

were also larger heating surface, larger cylinders and larger water tanks; and the locomotive crews were allowed cabs to shelter them from the extreme conditions of Mont Cenis.

As with locomotives, so with rolling stock: although the Midland Wagon Co. was willing to build, the order went to Chevalier, Cheilus & Cie of Paris. It included goods wagons and passenger coaches, some of which were to be on four wheels and some on six with radial axles. The Mont Cenis company's experience with Chevalier, however, was to be happier than with Gouin.

At the end of July 1866 J. B. Fell offered his resignation as Managing Director, which was accepted. He was, perhaps, financially embarrassed like so many others at that time, for there followed a period of acrimonious negotiation between him and the Mont Cenis company over payment of royalties for use of his patents. Earlier, it seems, it had been understood that use of these would be free of charge. Involved in this too was the Centre Rail Locomotive & Railway Co. Ltd., which Fell had set up to acquire his patent rights, with Brassey, Brogden, Alexander and Brunlees among its subscribers. But the agreement to buy the rights was not completed, and in June 1867 Fell wrote to Brassey that there had been so much misunderstanding that he proposed to dissolve it and form another company. This plan he carried out, for it was wound up in 1868, while in 1867 Fell had formed The Patent Centre Rail Co. Ltd - subscribers included Brunlees, Desbrière and Sir Cusack Roney, but not Brassey - to which he assigned his patents on 30 April 1868. Throughout all this, however, Fell remained a director of the Mont Cenis Railway Co. Ltd., and on occasion acted on its behalf.

By the beginning of September 1866 when Abinger, Brogden and Vallombrosa made a visit of inspection, 2,200 men were being employed; works on the French side were supervised by Brassey's agent Mr Blake. Rails were being laid at both ends of the line and on the plateau. There were some problems, of course. Gianoli's efforts were hampered by the scarcity of horses, which he needed to cart materials, caused by the war between Italy and Austria. On the French side, when attempts were made to put up the fence which was to keep road traffic off the railway, the foundation of the roadway was found to comprise stones so large that the post holes could be made only by blasting. But in general nothing, except perhaps the locomotives, seemed to prevent opening at the proper time, as Vallombrosa wrote to the Duke of Sutherland. 'If we have 7 years [of operation]' he added 'we shall have a very sound profit.' Such optimism was soon to receive a sharp setback.

It had been a cool summer and the snow and glaciers had not melted as much as usual, so that a few days of warm rain with a south wind caused extensive flooding. On 25 September, a tributary to the River Arc brought down so much debris from a ravine near Bramans that the river itself, already swollen, was blocked. The result was a reservoir which built up until its natural dam eventually burst. As Capt. Tyler was to put it in his third report 'The mass of water which then rolled down the valley carried all before it'.

Between St Michel and Termignon the imperial road, and the associated railway works, were damaged in fifty places. Of four km of line which had been laid only one remained, and two new bridges built to carry the railway were carried away. Brassey had the route inspected by Charles Jones (probably the same Charles Jones who was one of his agents on the *Meridionale*) and Jones reported that there were gaps in the road from 10 to 600 metres in length. He recommended that Brassey should undertake repairs for the French government. Since the road carried the supplies to the tunnel workings, he added: 'if it was thought necessary to paralyse the advancement...of the Mont Cenis Tunnel, [repairs to] certain portions of the...road could be retarded.'[21] This Machiavellian scheme does not seem to have been adopted, but repairs to the road were eventually undertaken by Brassey with Blake as his agent. To achieve the contract may have needed a personal approach by the Duke of Sutherland to the French emperor; it had still not been received by 20 December. Eventually, when the work was done, the opportunity was taken to improve gradients and curves, and massive retaining walls were built. A new iron bridge had to be built over the Arc at Pont de la Denise to replace one of the bridges which had been washed away. Repairing the damage to road and rail had put the railway project back by months.

Between Lanslebourg and Susa, however, the permanent way was mostly complete by early December 1866 when snow halted work for the winter. Sleepers were 3 feet apart, of larch and oak. The sleepers, or at least those eventually sold to the Lausanne-Echallens Railway, were only 1.5 m or even 1.45 m long. That is very short for the gauge, and might reflect the economic construction of a railway intended for a short life, and/or the limited

OPPOSITE PAGE
*One of the illustrations filed with Fell's third patent (no. 2174, provisional spec. Aug. 1866, complete spec. Feb. 1867) shows a locomotive apparently derived from no. 2, with improvements: overhang has been reduced by placing the rear axle below the firebox, and the rocking arms and their shafts to the rear of the cylinders, which in turn improves accessibility to the front cylinder covers. The design has been worked out in such detail as to lead to the suspicion that, had the locomotives been built in England, this might have been how they would have appeared.*
***Une des illustrations de la troisième invention breveté de Fell (no. 2174, spec. provisoire, août 1866, spec. complète février 1967) montre une version en apparence ameliorée de la locomotive no. 2: Le problème de la saillie a été resolu en plaçant l'essieu arrière sous le foyer et les leviers à bascule et leurs manches derrière les cylindres, ce qui rend les étuis des cylindres plus accessibles. Certains ont soupconné qui si les locomotives avaient été construites en Angleterre, elles seraient apparues comme telles.***
BY COURTESY OF THE MITCHELL LIBRARY, GLASGOW CITY LIBRARIES.

width of the railway's site. Some sleepers were evidently longer: Whymper and Couche include scale drawings of sleepers 6 ft 9 inches (about 2.06 m) and 2.15 m long respectively. Running rails were flat-bottom, weighed 30 kg per metre (about 60½ lb/yd), and 6.3 or 6.4m long; they were spiked direct to the sleepers. Centrally along the track, longitudinal timbers were bolted end-to-end to the sleepers: fastened to these at 3 feet intervals by coach screws were the wrought iron supports for the central rail. This was double-headed, laid on its side and fastened to the supports by bolts through the web; its centre line was 10½ inches above the running rails[22]. The central rail was provided wherever gradients were steep or curves were sharp, and extended, eventually, to some 30 miles of route; where it commenced, its ends were tapered.

Turntables were of cast iron and limited diameter.

Level crossings were numerous. Where the railway, at a level crossing, was so steep that the central rail was needed, the length over the crossing was carried on hinged supports and counter balanced. Normally it lay in a trough at about the same level as running rails and road surface; when a train was due, it was raised into position by a trackside lever, its downhill end abutting onto the end of the next fixed central rail. The uphill end was tapered vertically. Where a crossing was on a sharp curve, two successive lowering rails were provided.

The lowering rail device was the invention of Edmund Barnes, another native of Furness who had been appointed Locomotive Superintendent. The resident engineer was Valentine G. Bell, who had assisted Brunlees in laying out the line, and Desbrière had been appointed the company's agent in Paris where the locomotives and rolling stock were being built. By the summer of 1867 things were far enough advanced for Monsieur H. Gohierre to be appointed *Chef de l'Exploitation*.

The thousands of men who laboured on construction remain almost entirely anonymous. With one remarkable exception: Angelo Castagneri, who was one of a party of young Piedmontese employed on the French

side who were making their way home over a high col in October 1866. Castagneri is said to have slipped into a crevasse in a glacier and disappeared; his companions left him for dead. It was a week before his father, descending into the crevasse with a ladder, found him still alive and got him home. His frostbitten feet became gangrenous and dropped off, but Castagneri himself survived[23].

Shareholders, at the second half-yearly general meeting on 19 February 1867, were told that 'the greatest portion of the line' would be open in May. But on 4 March Fell wrote to the board that he anticipated opening in September. On 4 April, the board was considering the locations for locomotive sheds and repair shops. But construction of the locomotives themselves - at some stage their quantity was increased from ten to twelve - had fallen way behind schedule: the board now heard from Desbrière that the first locomotive was expected to be ready by 1 May, the second in June, with the others following once a week. The first carriage was ready except for its wheels. This progress was considered unsatisfactory, and Alexander, who was in attendance, was instructed to proceed at once to Paris.

His effectiveness, however, seems to have been limited, although the first carriage was completed in time for it to be exhibited, and admired, at the Paris Universal Exhibition in May. In the middle of August the Board of Trade eventually dispatched Captain Tyler for a third time, to re-inspect the railway over Mont Cenis and the progress of the tunnel. En route he inspected the locomotives and carriages still under construction in Paris, and when he commenced his inspection of the Mont Cenis Railway on 22 August the repairs to the line between St Michel and Lanslebourg were still incomplete[24].

Captain Tyler's arrival evidently spurred on those repairing the line to redouble their efforts, for the permanent way was complete enough for him to essay a trial trip on 26 August. (That is the date given in his official report, and elsewhere, although some press reports published soon afterwards gave the date of his trial trip as 21 August.) However, although the first of the Gouin locomotives, no. 3, had at last been delivered (and he had noted another at Culoz in course of delivery), it was 'hardly ready for the journey'. This was surely a diplomatic comment if ever there was one, in view of the troubles shortly to be reported with these locomotives. Anyway, Tyler was obliged to fall back on no. 2. It was said that no locomotive had travelled over the line before, so it sounds as though nos. 1 and 2 had been moved from the trial line down to St Michel, and there marooned by the floods. At any rate it was no. 2, coupled to a carriage and a wagon fitted with seats, which formed the first train over the Mont Cenis Railway: the first train ever to pass from France into Italy.

We are fortunate that a personal letter in which Alexander Brogden described the event to the Duke of Sutherland survives in the Sutherland records. He wrote:

> ...We left at 6.30 AM on Monday and went very carefully over the part of the line between Pont de la Denise and Modane as the works there had been constructed very recently and were not consolidated - nor even completely finished. After Modane up the incline toward the curves at the Fort Essilon we went at a moderate pace until we came to Termignon - there although the gradient is 1 in 13 the centre rails had not been laid and if the day had not been remarkably fine we should probably have not succeeded in getting further. We were all very anxious about it and not very certain - however we faced the hill and without once slipping we reached the top gaining steam and speed all the way. We could not help giving a cheer as we reached the top and then went along at a good speed to Lanslebourg. A triumphal arch had been erected and all the people turned out to see their old friend - Loco No 2. Leaving Lanslebourg we had a little difficulty with the points but that was soon overcome and we started very gallantly for the summit - without slip or jar or hindrance of any kind we went on - stopping once for water (which might have been dispensed with) and reached the summit in 45 minutes.
>
> There Gianoli had provided Dejeuner and we stayed some time - started again away Capt.

Tyler calling out *à voitures Messieurs pour Italie* - all went well and smoothly and we reached the Grand Croix where the steep inclines begin. Here we had a little bad driving and at one moment furiously and then were pulled up quite short but as soon as the break *(sic)* arrangements were organised we went down smoothly enough - the Duke of Vallombrosa sitting on the Buffer and all of us sitting or standing on the Engine where we could find a place. It was a beautiful sight - one instant on the verge of a precipice with the valley thousands of feet below us then plunging into covered way or tunnel and out again into the warm sunny air with the plains and valley at our feet. Everything went very well and we reached Susa at a good speed but at every moment under control.

> I assure you we were all much pleased & not the least the Duke and Capt. Tyler. We...drank sundry bumpers in loyal and characteristic toasts. The inhabitants of Susa must have thought us all jolly good fellows as the chorus was repeated at almost every toast. Tyler distinguished himself by composing a song & we have scarcely been able to keep him from sending it to *The Times*...

We can find out a little more about this remarkable occasion from a newspaper, *The Reporter or London Monetary Times*, quoting *Railway News* held in the same collection[25]. (It was also reported in *The Times* 28 August and 2 September 1867 and *The Engineer* 30 August 1867.) There were about 50 people on the train, and the driver was James Brunlees himself. From Susa 'the scream of the engine whistle could be heard, and the train seen, when yet far up the height', so for miles before the train reached the town it passed through lines of cheering men, women and children. With Fell and Brogden as well as Vallombrosa riding on the front of the engine, the train entered the station yard at Susa at five o'clock 'amid the thunder of cannon and the shouts of assorted thousands'.

'The following impromptu' the newspaper adds 'was sung by Capt Tyler...cordially accompanied in the choruses by the party who had made the memorable journey with him:

AIR: "I'm Afloat"

The Alps have succumbed to the skill of Brunlees
Six thousand seven hundred feet mounted with ease
The engine of Fell in Italia you see
We have crossed, we have crossed, o'er the great Mont Cenis.

Sharp curves and steep gradients may add to the load,
The snow and the ice may encumber the road
The precipice yawns, and mists hinder the sight
But with wheels on the central rail safely we bite.

CHORUS -
The Alps have succumbed to the skill of Brunlees
Bell, Blake, Derbyshire, Baylis are now at their ease
Alexander and Barnes may be now at their ease
Six thousand seven hundred feet mounted with ease
The engine of Fell in Italia you see.

Then a bumper outpour to the Fell centre rail,
Vallombrosa and Brogden, directors, all hail,
To Brassey, Zenolli ['Gianoli', presumably, is meant], to all by whose aid
This Mont Cenis Rail has been skilfully laid

CHORUS - The Alps etc.

There is but one providence, His guiding will
Directeth what time and space railways shall fill.
Thanks to Him for his grace! On this work, in His sight,
May England, France, Italy peacefully unite.

CHORUS -
We have crossed o'er the summit of great Mont Cenis
We have crossed, we have crossed, o'er the great Mont Cenis
We have crossed, we have crossed, we have crossed Mont Cenis.'

Somehow the rousing cheer that must have accompanied that final chorus comes echoing down the years!

And after that, so hardy were Victorians, the party embarked in road vehicles to return over Mont Cenis, travelling all night to catch the early train from St Michel.

The first crossing of the Mont Cenis by train had come not a moment too soon.

Another Alpine crossing by railway, over the Brenner Pass, had been opened a few days earlier. Of much more concern to the Mont Cenis promoters, however, was progress with the Mont Cenis Tunnel. Brogden, in the letter quoted above, continued by describing how he had accompanied Captain Tyler into the tunnel. The tunnellers had good ventilation and the 'boring engines' worked very rapidly. 'I think' he added 'all the estimates we have had of its completion are fallacious - and I see no reason why it should not be pierced in 3 years and completed in 4 years.' The railway approach on the French side was, perhaps fortunately, another matter - there was no prospect of the works being commenced for a year, and they would then take four years to complete.

His figures probably came from Tyler, for they appear in Tyler's report on this visit. He gives the lengths then bored: on the Italian side, 4,490 m., and on the French side (where the tunnellers had passed through the quartz and were back in schist), 2,876 m. That made the total 7,366 m, so there remained to be pierced 4,884 m.

On the Mont Cenis Railway itself there was still much to be done - completing laying the central rail, ballasting, establishing watering places and a telegraph, completing the stations. But locomotives and rolling stock were now arriving, and the company felt confident enough to ask for official Franco-Italian government inspection on 20 September, with a view to opening as soon as possible after that for freight, and for passengers in October.

The 20 September date proved premature, but on 11 October Fell wrote from his home in Furness to the Duke of Sutherland. He enclosed a copy of a report by Gouin's foreman to his employer, which described a highly successful run late in September with no. 3 from St Michel to the Col du Mont Cenis and back. On the ascent from Lanslebourg to the summit, a speed of 15 kph had been maintained without over heating the motion; the train on this section comprised six wagons laden with rails, other materials and 'une grande quantité de voyageurs'.

At this period it was Thomas Brassey's practice to make a tour of his contracts on the Continent every spring and autumn, passing over the Mont Cenis en route, and so in October he duly arrived at St Michel. No doubt he expected to repeat the triumph that had attended Tyler's visit but when, on 12 October, he attempted to take a train over to Susa, the result was a disaster (Brogden was there and wrote to the duke about it on 19 October). The train included seven wagons, one fourgon and three carriages with about 30 passengers, a very big load. By Fourneax the locomotive was in a bad state and obliged to go slowly; it then failed completely, for a rocking shaft had broken. Another locomotive was following: this was tried but failed similarly. One member of the party later claimed that three locomotives were tried one after another, and each became incapacitated[26]. Helps, in his biography of Brassey, describes this as the opening of the Fell railway, and no doubt that was what Brassey had expected to attend, though on the day it must have been evident that opening had been deferred. The fine August weather of Tyler's visit had given way to premature winter with a bitter north-east wind. Helps has Brassey, disappointed and vexed, standing about in the cold and wet while a replacement locomotive is obtained, and from this developing a chill which led to fever and in turn to ill-health which eventually proved fatal.

What the shareholders were told, in the directors' report to a general meeting on 26 November 1867, was that during the trial trips some of the materials used to build the engines failed, being of inferior quality, and that opening must be deferred. The failures, the directors were at pains to point out, did not relate to the central rail: on that, the locomotives worked well. The rather desperate expedient of extending the central rail over the entire line was being considered. By that date five locomotives had been delivered by Gouin, three more were ready for delivery, two were far advanced and the remaining two being built.

In the locomotives, apart from a generally poor standard of workmanship - about which Alexander had complained while the locomotives were being built, without being able to persuade Gouin's men to change their accustomed ways - two main faults had emerged.

The first lay with the trailing axles, with which the first three locomotives had been built. According to Tyler, in his third report, these were fitted with 'yielding axleboxes'. But evidently they did not yield enough, for the locomotives would not go round the curves. Provision of flexibility in locomotive wheelbases was still in its infancy.

The solution was to eliminate the trailing wheels. This of course threw an added load onto the rear driving wheels: they had to be fitted with additional bearings and springs, no easy task in a location already so crowded.

The second fault related to the rocking shafts, which despite being of 5 inches diameter at the bearings were clearly unable to withstand the stresses to which they were subjected. The specification had required them to be made from forged steel, or from iron of the first quality. Iron had been used, seemingly of indifferent quality, for those shafts which broke showed extensive flaws. Others were said to have twisted. There were also imperfections in the layout of the drive to the vertical wheels, of which little was immediately said: they are mentioned here in chapter six.

The cure adopted was to replace the shafts by shafts of steel, and 7 inches diameter[27]. This took months: Barnes, when responding on 5 February 1868 to a string of detailed enquiries from Brassey about progress, wrote that he was still waiting for them - but on 17 April *The Times* was able to report that there were seven locomotives at St Michel, in which the rocking shafts had either been replaced or were on the point of being so.

The Gouin locomotives were also notorious, when new, for running their bearings hot.

All this is rather at variance with the report by Gouin's foreman mentioned above. Maybe he had spent the month, between No. 3's arrival and the run described, in removing the trailing axle and sorting out the bearings.

As for rolling stock, Chevalier gave no cause for complaint about quality, but their ideas on delivery times seem to have been as elastic as Gouin's. In March 1867 Fell had written to the board that they had promised to deliver the four-wheeled carriages and wagons by the end of May, and the six-wheeled ones by the end of June. So far as wagons are concerned, when Brogden wrote to the duke on 29 August all had arrived at St Michel and were being erected. As for the coaches, on 5 February 1868 Barnes wrote to Brassey that he had received two 1st class carriages, with nine still to come; three 2nd class, with two to come; and three 3rd class, with five to come. He had however, received 103 wagons.

When the railway eventually opened in June 1868 *The Engineer* reported that it had: seven 1st class carriages, each seating 12 passengers; four 2nd class, each seating 14; eight 3rd class, each seating 16; four luggage vans; and 95 wagons, various[28]. Although the company was said to be fully supplied with rolling stock, it is evident that the six-wheelers had still not arrived - or, if they had, they were not being put into service. They were eventually operated, for Fell himself stated in 1870[29] that they had been found to run more steadily, and with less resistance on the sharp curves, than the four-wheelers.

Every vehicle, it seems, was equipped with horizontal guide wheels bearing on the central rail, and with brakes on the vertical wheels and on the central rail. The carriages had a balcony at one end where the brakesman rode, and passengers got on and off; seats were longitudinal, facing inwards, and there were doors in each end of the coach and in the balustrade of the balcony, with a folding iron footway between coaches.

Concurrently with these long delays in getting its railway opened, the company had been experiencing further financial problems. In March 1867 the board agreed to seek a loan of £60,000 against guarantees by the directors. On 12 September *The Times* announced that subscriptions were invited for £125,000 in 7 per cent debentures, adding that the line would probably open in October. The invitation went unheeded by the investing public, perhaps because the interest rate was too low: in their report to the shareholders' meeting on 26 November the directors stated that no applications had been received. In that report, no chairman is named - Hudson is omitted - and Crampton too has disappeared from the list of directors. Meanwhile, in writing to the duke on 11 October, Fell had said that Brassey had guaranteed £15,000 needed for the works.

The meeting of 26 November authorised an increase in the company's borrowing powers from £125,000 to £202,600, and payment of interest at 10 per cent. At that date its liabilities were stated to be £182,584; although £149,850 had been raised from issue of shares, only £2,600 had been raised from debentures. It was decided to make a full issue of bonds, that is £200,000 at 10 per cent; the directors agreed to subscribe for £150,000 on condition the other shareholders subscribed £50,000. If the bonds were not taken up within fourteen days, the works of the line were liable to be sold in discharge of the liabilities (with an opportunity, perhaps to buy them back from the creditors). That did not happen but neither, probably, were all the bonds taken up. On 18 January 1868 George Loch, the Duke of Sutherland's agent - concerned, perhaps, that his master's enthusiasm for such a project went beyond the bounds of financial prudence - was writing to him busily rubbishing the undertaking. Further foreign creditors had been found, increasing the liabilities to £243,000. Eventually, after Abinger and Cutbill had called on Loch more than once, the duke provided £22,000.

The line itself, the directors reported in November 1867, was complete except for St Michel and Susa stations and a very small part of the covered ways. That small part was soon increased, for snow slips carried away more than 100 m of them. In the early part of 1868 no. 2 was hard at work on the Italian side, conveying materials for repair and extension of the covered ways, and the occasional unofficial passenger as well.

By then Barnes had in his employment 25 men including four good engine drivers, all

British; six fitters employed on locomotive work; three blacksmiths and strikers making points and crossings; and one fitter, one smith and one striker on wagon work. His department's accomodation at St Michel included running shed, fitting shop, smiths' shop and carriage shed; a coke shed and materials store were still required. At Susa there were a running shed and a coke shed.

On 21 February, *The Times* reported that the railway was expected to open on 1 May, once again without result. With opening so often reported as imminent, and so often deferred, people began to wonder whether it ever would open, whether the whole thing was a hoax, or at best a failure.

At last efforts of Barnes and his fitters bore fruit. On 20 April, one of the locomotives took a trial train with a load of 25 tons from St Michel to Susa; it returned the following day. On 23 April, another locomotive made the return journey within the day, and ran the

length of the line in 5½ hours, including one hour of stoppages[30].

Official inspection of the line by a Franco-Italian commission followed very quickly: the commissioners left St Michel by special train on 28 April, stayed overnight at Modane after visiting the tunnel workings, and continued to Susa on 29 April, stopping almost every mile to inspect the line. The French commissioners returned over the line on 2 May[31]. In the commissioners' report the only specific improvement demanded seems to have been interlocking of signals with the lowering central rail at three of the level crossings: once this was done, the line could be opened for goods traffic, and, after continuous operation for fifteen days, for passengers.

That fifteen-day trial period was completed, according to *Engineering* of 19 June 1869, on Tuesday 2 June by which date one train had operated in each direction, without accident, each day during the fifteen

*On 1 February 1868, when the much-postponed opening of the MCR had still to happen, the* ILLUSTRATED LONDON NEWS *none the less provided readers with this spirited portrayal of a train comprising no. 2 locomotive and two coaches.*

**Le 1er février 1868, lorsque l'inauguration tardive du CF du Mont Cenis n'avait pas encore eu lieu, le journal illustré 'Illustrated London News' offrait à ses lecteurs cette image dynamique de la locomotive no. 2 et ses deux voitures.**

days ending on that day. From this, if Sunday working was included, it appears that the Mont Cenis Railway was opened for goods traffic on 19 May 1868 - or, if the line was not operated on Sundays, on 16 May. Or again, perhaps only when it eventually opened for passengers: *Engineering* calls the trial trains 'experimental running' and traffic receipts seem only to have been recorded from the date of opening to passengers. But it is difficult to imagine the company, once it had authorisation to carry goods, turning away any traffic that was offered.

By mid-May the company's promoters had started to gather at Mont Cenis for a celebration. The Duke of Sutherland travelled over the line for the first time on 15 May. His pocket diary survives[32], though the entries are of the briefest. 'Leave Paris' he noted for 14 May, and, for 15 May: 'Cross the Hill. Sleep Turin'. He went on to visit Leghorn and

Florence before coming back to Turin. The duke was, perhaps, the first British tourist visiting Italy to travel out and back via France by rail throughout, apart from the Channel crossing. On 23 May he notes: 'Leave Turin by special. Cross Hill'.

At Susa he was met by Brassey and Brunlees who had travelled out from London taking 35 hours for the journey, including the MCR. Helps, regrettably, omitted to mention this successful return visit in his biography of Brassey. For the celebratory journey to St Michel they were joined by most people of importance in the project: Blount, Brogden, Buddicom, Fell, Cutbill, Bell, Blake, Alexander, Barnes, Gohierre, Desbrière, Crampton, Count Arrivabene and Signor Milla the Italian government commissioner. Present too were representatives of *The Times*[33], doubtless Frederick Hardman, and the *Morning Post*[34]. The chief manager of the *Alta*

*Italia* railway, unable to be present, sent a message of support, assuring the company of co-operation. The party in total numbered 54.

They embarked at Susa in a train comprising a locomotive (driver, Tom Morton), four 1st class carriages and a van, which left at 11.30. The day was beautiful and hot, and the mountains seen at their best: the lower slopes rich with the bright green foliage of early summer, the upper pastures blue with Gentians, the peaks still covered with fast-disappearing snow. Delight was tempered only by passage of the covered ways, stifling hot and resembling a vapour bath. Openings were being cut. During the descent of a 1 in 12 gradient at 12 mph, at a signal from the duke the brakes were applied fully: the train was found to halt within half a minute and 36 yards. The train reached St Michel about 4.30 pm, and after a most agreeable excursion, the travellers continued their celebrations over a convivial dinner at the Hôtel de la Poste. The public opening of the line was announced for 8 June.

It seemed certain, but once again it did not happen. *Engineering*, represented no doubt by editor Zerah Colburn, arrived for that date and found opening again deferred[35]. He was allowed to travel on 8 June on a special, comprised of a locomotive, a 1st class coach

and two wagons loaded with material for stations and so on. The locomotive was no. 14 which had just been delivered, completing Gouin's order. Colburn is noteworthy at this period for writing which is as unfavourable to Fell as it is favourable to Robert Fairlie[36]: the Mont Cenis Railway, he wrote, could have been as well worked without the central rail, by use of Fairlie's steam carriages. But having travelled over it, he cannot resist starting to enthuse: 'a very bold engineering work ...enterprise and skill...'.

This latest delay, it seemed, had been caused 'by some difficulty in arranging with the French and Italian railway companies respecting the times at which the trains should be run'. Since the *Alta Italia* had already promised support, this reads as if the PLM was still dragging its feet. But relations with the *Alta Italia* were to have ups and downs too.

Eventually, on 15 June 1868 at 7.20 in the morning[37] and apparently without ceremony, the first passenger train headed out of Susa, and up over the hill. The Mont Cenis Railway was open for passengers at last.

By 1 April, a total of 8,159 metres of the Mont Cenis Tunnel had been bored, with 4,061 metres to go: when the summit railway opened, in other words, two thirds of the tunnel had already been completed.

CHAPTER FOUR

# OPEN AT LAST

It had taken far longer to build the railway than anticipated, but the cost of building it and equipping it was remarkably close to the estimate. The figure of £392,026 16s 0d[38] works out at £7,966 8s 1d a mile - Brunlees had estimated £8,000.

What had shareholders got for their money, and what did passengers find? By correlating several contemporary accounts of the railway and a few later ones[39], we can get a fair idea of it - although inevitably there are inconsistencies. Remarkably the lists of stations vary quite a lot: I suspect that several of the small stations were originally planned as water stops only, but were eventually used by passengers. The station buildings were of the simplest.

Passengers arriving by the PLM at St Michel found themselves already encircled by mountains. The Mont Cenis train was waiting across the platform for passengers and mails: assuming the line here had been built as planned, the MCR's running line and loop were tucked in between the standard gauge and the north bank of the River Arc. During the floods there had been fears, fortunately unfounded, that they would be washed away. The train, to judge by photographs, usually comprised a Gouin locomotive, a *fourgon* (ie, a guard's & luggage van), a goods van, and three coaches. A passenger on the third day of operation[40] found that the train crew totalled five: as well as the driver and fireman, there were a chief guard and two brakesmen on the train, distributed one to a coach. This was in the days before continuous brakes were usual. It was reading of the use of pneumatic tools in boring the Mont Cenis Tunnel - and,

*A timing diagram - blank, unfortunately - for the 'Chemin de Fer du Mont-Cenis' survives among the Sutherland papers.* **Un graphique de marche pour le Chemin de Fer du Mont Cenis - malheureusement vierge-retrouvé parmi les papiers du Duc de Sutherland.** STAFFORDSHIRE RECORD OFFICE.

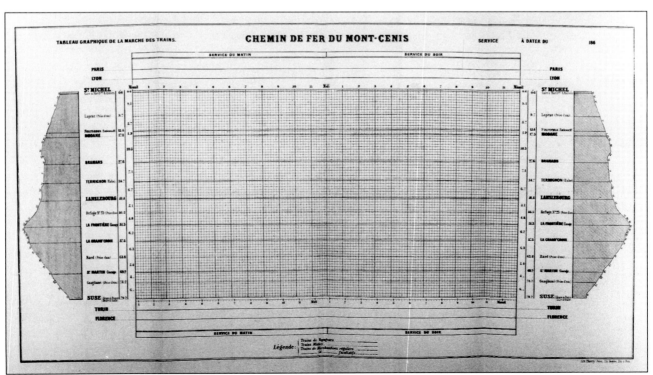

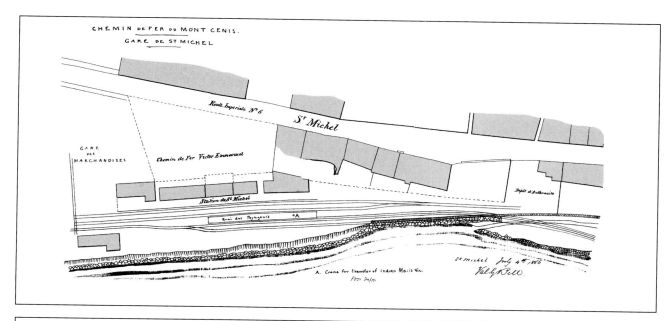

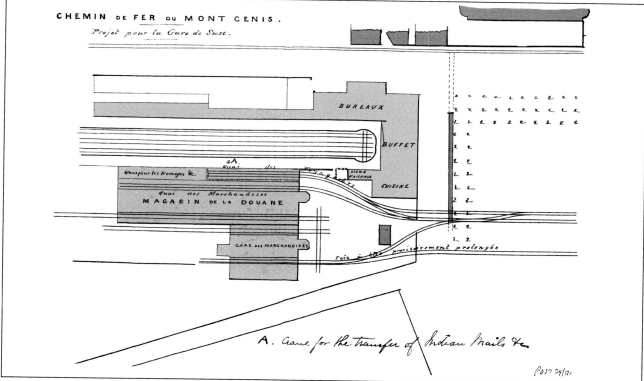

*Drawings, which were attached to Capt. Tyler's 1866 report to indicate arrangements for transfer of the Indian mails at St Michel and Susa, show the proposed layouts for tracks and other facilities at these stations. In the drawing of Susa, north is at its foot and the MCR approaches from the right. The dual-gauge track is noteworthy.*

**Ces dessins, appartenant au rapport du Capitaine Tyler en 1866, indiquant les demarches de transfer du courrier indien à St Michael et à Suse, montrent le tracé de la voie ferrée et autres services dans ces gares. Sur le dessin de Suse, le nord est au bas de la page et le CF du Mont Cenis emerge à droite.L' écartement mixte de la voie ferrée est particulièrement intéressant.**

POST OFFICE ARCHIVES REF. POST 29/131.

*The Fell railway at Lanslebourg.*
**Le chemin de fer de Fell à Lanslebourg.**
MUSÉES D'ART ET D'HISTOIRE DE CHAMBÉRY.

particularly, of how compressed air was supplied to them through 3,000 feet of piping - that gave George Westinghouse the idea of using compressed air to operate continuous brakes down the length of a railway train.

St Michel goods station and workshops were not at the passenger station, but 30 chains (0.6 km) up the line. Here too, presumably, were the locomotive and carriage sheds.

From St Michel to Lanslebourg the railway followed the Maurienne, the valley of the River Arc. This provided a generally steady ascent interrupted by steeper pitches, to surmount which the central rail was installed. Thus the departure from St Michel on a gradient of 1 in 50 was followed by a mile of 1 in 20, where trains first encountered the central rail. Beyond, a series of sharp curves led to a bridge over the river. The south bank was then followed for about $1\frac{1}{2}$ miles to the Pont de la Denise, a plate girder bridge of 112 feet span and 24 feet width, which carried both railway and Imperial road over the Arc. The north bank was followed until the Pont de Chevies returned the line to the south bank shorly before Lapraz (modern spelling, La Praz). Here, at 6 miles 2 chains (9.7 km) from St Michel were station and water crane. Water cranes came frequently on the MCR: on a central-rail railway the weight of water in a

locomotive's tanks was not needed for adhesion, and it was by contrast advantageous to minimise the weight of water carried.

At Fourneaux (9 m 45 ch.; 15.4 km) came the workings for the French end of the tunnel. The actual entrance was some 350 feet above the MCR, but the line passed close by the compressor house containing the water-powered air compressors. The timing diagram reproduced as an illustration on page 46 indicates '*Embranch¹*', i.e. 'junction, branch line', which suggests there was a siding or sidings for delivery of materials to the tunnellers. Not far beyond came the little town of Modane (10 m 60 ch.; 17.3 km) with its station, from which passengers could see the first stretch of 1 in 12 right ahead and be suitably impressed - although westbound passengers seem to have been even more impressed when looking back and seeing what their train had just descended.

Some $3\frac{1}{2}$ miles further on where the valley narrowed passengers saw, prominent in an elevated position on the far side of the river, the fortifications of L'Esseillon - built earlier in the century by the Sardinian monarchy for defence against the French, and so since 1860 partly dismantled but still imposing. A short length of down gradient followed, at 1 in $45\frac{1}{2}$. The railway traversed several sharp-radius curves with the track on the edge of a precipice high above the torrent: the central rail was provided for lateral security, and for travellers' peace of mind. On such curves, the wheels and rails together gave out a shrill metallic sound like the whistle of a distant train.

The village of Bramans (17 m 12 ch., 27.6 km) had station and water crane; the railway crossed the river yet again and came to the village of Termignon (21 m 45 ch., 34.7 km) where it was equipped similarly. The name indicates the termination of the valley, that is of Maurienne; certainly the continuation of the railway could be spied some 300 feet above, on the hillside to the right. It achieved that position by temporarily deserting the road and taking a great loop round a side-

valley to the north, climbing throughout at 1 in 14.3. Having re-gained the upper valley of the Arc, it was then able to descend at 1 in 33 for a couple of miles.

Lanslebourg (25 m 58 ch., 41.4 km) was both the principal intermediate station and, in operating terms, the mid-point of the line. Trains halted for fifteen minutes while engines were changed. The station was in front of an immense range of buildings constructed as barracks during the time of Napoleon I and latterly used as stabling for the diligence horses. There were sidings, turntable and engine shed.

Leaving Lanslebourg railway and road had to forsake the valley of the Arc which they had followed for so long. Crossing the river for

*Continuous snowshed of timber and corrugated iron protected the Fell railway where it snaked its way down from the eastern edge of the plateau. The railway can also be seen descending the mountain side at 1 in 14 in the middle distance.*

**Le Chemin de Fer du Mont Cenis était protégé sur son parcours du versant est du plateau par un abri anti-neige en bois et en tôle.**
MUSÉES D'ART ET D'HISTOIRE DE CHAMBÉRY.

the last time, they turned through 45 degrees and headed up the mountainside towards the col, the lowest point on the ridge. For six miles up through the zig-zags to the railway's summit the climb was continuous: the easiest gradient was 1 in 19.23, the steepest 1 in 12.5. Viewers in Lanslebourg could follow the progress of a train by observing puffs of smoke rise above the pine trees, advancing alternately from right to left, then from left to right, and ever higher. To a passenger in the train, Lanslebourg seemed to descend without receding. About half-way up, at the roadside travellers' refuge no. 23 (28 m 71 ch., 46.5 km), uphill trains halted to take water. The covered ways commenced, becoming longer and more frequent with increasing altitude. Eventually at the col the line reached its summit at the station of La Frontière (31 m 70

ch., 51.3 km): the frontier itself was marked by a large stone with 'France' inscribed on one side and 'Italia' on the other.

Now the line was able to descend comparatively gently across the summit plateau between the high mountains, past Alpine meadows and shepherds' huts and Lake Cenis which was said to produce excellent trout for six months of the year, and to be frozen over for the rest. The hospice was passed on the left - some accounts put a station here - and the station and watering point of La Grand' Croix (35 m 58 ch., 57.5 km) soon followed.

Then the descent began in earnest, all the way to Susa and never less steep than 1 in 25 and mostly in the range 1 in 12 to 1 in 14. Here too began the most extensive series of covered ways and avalanche shelters: in total,

*Whymper's engraving of Les Echelles, the zig-zags by which the road descended from the eastern side of the piateau. The railway, diverging from the road to follow its earlier, more easily graded but more avalanche-prone route, can be seen in the background.*

**Une gravure des Echelles de Whymper: zig-zags de la route, le long du versant est du plateau. On peut voir, au fond, le chemin de fer qui s'écarte de la route pour suivre son chemin précédent, moins en pente, mais plus enclin aux avalanches.**

*Les Echelles seen in 1995 from Whymper's viewpoint. The two buildings still stand and the course of the railway can be discerned. The avalanche shelter where it leaves the road (see also p. 7) is more prominent than in Whymper's day, when a timber-and-iron snowshed butted up against its entrance.*

**Les Echelles en 1995. Les deux batiments existent toujours, et le parcours du chemin de fer est encore visible.**

AUTHOR.

*The descent towards Bard was one of the few places on the Italian side of the pass where the Fell railway was located along the outer edge of the road.*
*__La descente vers Bard était un des rares endroits, du côté italien du col, ou le Chemin de Fer de Fell suivant la partie extérieure de la route.__*
MUSÉES D'ART ET D'HISTOIRE DE CHAMBÉRY.

some six miles of the line were covered over. It rapidly became evident that they had been built too low, that when upward trains were passing through the smoke and steam could not disperse. Conditions were well nigh intolerable,'worse than the Metropolitan', wrote a correspondent in *The Times* of 18 August 1868. (The underground Metropolitan Railway had been opened in 1863.) More openings had to be made. To protect passengers from the heat, trains were marshalled with the *fourgon* between the locomotive and the coaches.

In his *Scrambles amongst the Alps...* Edward Whymper recorded a driver's opinion, allegedly verbatim: ' "Yes, mister, they told us as how the line was very steep; but they didn't say that the engine would be on one curve, when the fourgon was on another, and the carriages was on a third. Them gradients

too...I think they are one in *ten*,... and they didn't say as how we was to come down them in that snakewise fashion. It's worse than the G.I.P., there a fellow could jump off; but here, in them covered ways, there ain't no place to jump to." ' The G.I.P., explained Whymper, was the Great Indian Peninsula Railway with its Bhore Ghaut incline.

But the eastbound passenger had his reward. Even Zerah Colburn forgot to carp: 'While passing through the covered way, occasional tantalising glimpses are obtained...of the landscape below; but once completely clear of it, there bursts into view a panorama which is simply magnificent'[41]. Far beneath lay the valley, deep, wide and fertile, dotted with villages and vineyards, with Susa, more than half a mile below, at its mouth and the plains of Piedmont beyond.

Towards Susa then the line wound along

the mountainsides, steadily dropping while the climate became ever warmer and the vegetation more lush. Bard station (39 m 51 ch., 63.8 km) was a water stop for upward trains, and was followed by stations at San Martino (43 m, 69.2 km), called St Martin in French, and Giaglione (45 m 38 ch., 73.2 km, French: Geaglioné) which again was a water stop on the way up. Finally the train ran into Susa (French: Suse) passing the locomotive and carriage sheds to reach the standard gauge terminus (49 m 17 ch., 79.2 km). Once again there appears to have been cross-platform interchange for passengers and mails. A large transhipment shed and customs house was provided, and there was mixed-gauge track in the yard.

The initial timetable had trains departing from Susa at 7.20 am and 8.30 am; for the latter, a connection had left Turin at 5.30 am. These trains were scheduled to arrive at St Michel at 11.45 am and 12.55 pm respectively; because there was a difference of 50 minutes between Italian time and French time, the actual journey time was scheduled at 5¼ hours. Return trains were scheduled to leave St Michel at 1.15 pm and 3.55 pm, and allowed the same length of time for the journey.

On the opening day the 7.20 comprised one 1st, one 2nd and one 3rd class carriage with two fourgons; the three coaches of the 8.30 were all 1st class, again with two fourgons; the first train was five minutes early into St Michel, the second two minutes.

Travelling by the train saved six hours over the diligence, the coaches were more spacious and comfortable, and the fare, even 1st class, was 20 francs cheaper. On the first day 29

*From June 1868 until December 1870 the MCR's weekly traffic receipts were reported in THE TIMES with sufficient regularity to be shown as a graph. The effects of floods, snow and the Franco-Prussian war are clearly shown. Where no figure is shown for a particular week, either it was not reported, or perhaps escaped the attention of the indexers*
**De juin 1868 à décembre 1870, les recettes du trafic hebdomadaire du CF du Mont Cenis étaint annoncées dans le 'Times'. Les dégâts causés par les innondations, la neige et la guerre franco-prussienne apparaissent très clairement. Un chiffre hebdomadaire absent indique qu'il n'avait pas été signalé ou répertorié.**
AUTHOR.

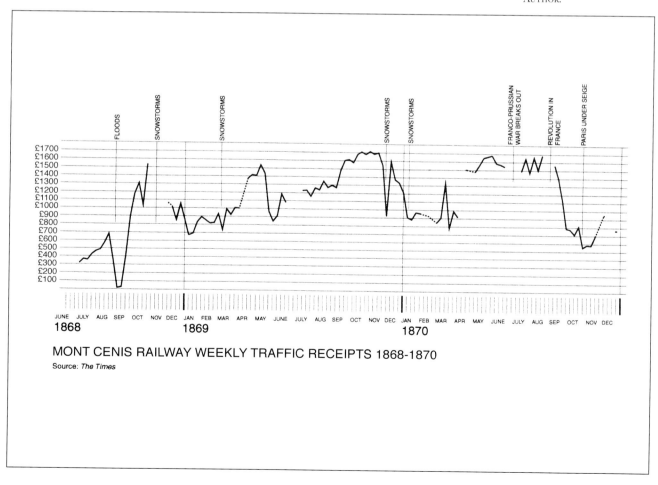

MONT CENIS RAILWAY WEEKLY TRAFFIC RECEIPTS 1868-1870
Source: *The Times*

*Gouin locomotive no. 10 heads a train comprising fourgon, van, two second or third class carriages and a first class carriage at the rear.*
**La locomotive Gouin no. 10 tire un train se composant d'un fourgon, d'un wagon couvert, de deux voitures de deuxième ou troisième classe et d'une voiture de première classe à l'arrière.**
COLLECTION K. CLINGAN.

passengers arrived at St Michel by the PLM, and 24 of them went forward by Mont Cenis train; the other five still preferred the diligence. The diligence services were soon reduced, although despite earlier forecasts they were not totally withdrawn: a single diligence was still crossing the pass daily in 1871, carrying at the most a dozen passengers each way.

The ordinary mails were carried by the MCR from its opening, initially without any saving in overall time, but it was soon arranged that schedules would be re-arranged from 1 August to provide improved connections between the MCR and the French and Italian Railways. This enabled letters from England to be delivered in Florence a day earlier. Through bookings for passengers were arranged from the same date.

This promising start was interrupted when once again storms and bad weather took a hand. Many of the Alpine passes were damaged that August and Mont Cenis was no exception. On 10 August a torrential rainstorm washed away a length of road between St Martin and Bard, leaving the rails suspended in the air. Pending repairs, trains worked to either side of the gap, which passengers had to struggle past on foot. But this incident was soon overshadowed by an even more serious one. On the night of 17-18 August the Arc rose up in flood again and by morning the Pont de la Denise was washed away. Elsewhere two embankments had been breached, and the PLM line had been seriously damaged between St Michel and St Jean de Maurienne.

Damage to the Pont de la Denise was proved not, however, to be due entirely to natural causes: a little way upstream, close to where a tunnel was being excavated for the eventual standard gauge railway, a bank of spoil had been allowed to spread out into the river. This had deflected the full force of the current, and rocks brought down with it, against one of the abutments of the bridge.

The immediate response was to put a temporary footbridge across the river. Pont de la Denise became the western terminus of the Fell railway, and from the other side of the river diligences carried passengers to and from St Jean. Road and rail had been repaired sufficiently for services to recommence in this way on 5 September. A replacement bridge for road and rail was built in time for the MCR to be reopened to St Michel about 28 September. But the PLM was in no hurry to complete repairs to its line, and for several more weeks, apparently, diligences filled the gap between St Michel and St Jean.

The PLM at this period was ready to use any excuse to send passengers for Italy via Marseilles rather than Mont Cenis, even, it was alleged, to giving out false information that the MCR was blocked[42]. It had little success: autumn was a popular time for visiting Italy and traffic over the Mont Cenis Railway was brisk, even while the rail route was interrupted. Trains had to be double-headed from Lanslebourg up to La Frontière.

Among the travellers were some V.I.Ps: Prince Arthur, third son of Queen Victoria, and the military hero Lord Napier of Magdala, who had just commanded the succesful expeditionary force to release the British Consul imprisoned in Abyssinia: a ten-mile broad gauge temporary military railway had been built in its support. Probably the most important to the MCR however was Lord Mayo who, en route to India to take up the post of viceroy, took the opportunity to try out the Brindisi route for himself. Fell accompanied him over the Mont Cenis and, with carriage of the Indian Mail still no more than an ambition, the MCR staff were clearly put on their mettle. The journey from St Michel to Susa was accomplished in a running time of 3 hours 45 minutes.

Recent continental publications mention a visit by the Prince of Wales, but I have found no contemporary reference to this and am inclined to suspect confusion with Prince Arthur.

While these troubles and triumphs had been going on in public, there had been other problems behind the scenes. Not only did the railway lack a general manager with overall responsibility on the spot - it seems to have been in charge of Blount, far away in Paris - but its two principal officials, Gohierre and

Barnes, had found it impossible to work in harmony. In these circumstances, much was wanting in the day to day running and maintenance of the railway. The board's solution - probably, in truth, Brassey's solution - was to send J. A. Longridge to inspect the railway and then, on 4 September, to appoint him a director with, in effect, full charge of it.

James Atkinson Longridge (1817-1896) came of a lineage which in railway terms was most distinguished, for his father was Michael Longridge, associate of George Stephenson, to whom he himself had been apprenticed. A varied career in railway engineering - mostly overseas - had taken him to Mauritius in 1858 where he laid out a railway system and in due course became Brassey's agent for construction. Useful experience for Mont Cenis, his responsibilities included working ballast trains over 1 in 27 gradients. While running the Mont Cenis Railway, he lived for much of the time in Savoy at Chambéry; he took with him his son, Michael Longridge (1847-1928). Just down from Cambridge, the young man must have found Mont Cenis a formative experience - particularly for one who would eventually become a distinguished president of the Institution of Mechanical Engineers.

Longridge's presence, the staff changes which he made (though Gohierre and Barnes kept their jobs, at least for the time being), and the improved accounting which he introduced, seem to have had a very beneficial effect. The most serious problem, however, was once again the state of the locomotives. Longridge in a letter to Brassey dated 23 September wrote that new cranks were to be put on ten disabled engines[43]. These appear to have been the offset cranks which drove the linkage coupling the horizontal wheels on either side of the central rail[44]. One wonders whether the clerk who copied out Longridge's letter had got the quantity of locomotives correct; if so, the work must have been done quickly, to judge from the traffic being carried. On 16 October, however, Cutbill reported to the Duke of Sutherland that four locomotives had recently broken down, two from failure of the offset cranks and two from breakage of the

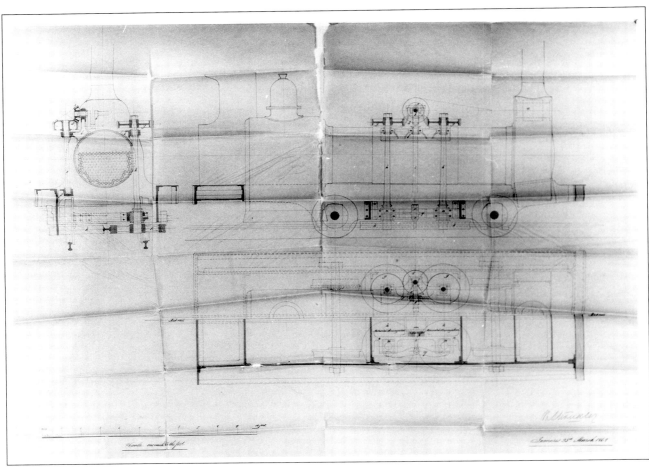

*In 1868 William Stroudley designed a locomotive intended for the Mont Cenis Railway and sent details to the Duke of Sutherland: he envisaged driving the horizontal wheels from cylinders placed above the smokebox.*

**En 1868, William Stroudley a dessiné une locomotive pour le Chemin de Fer du Mont Cenis et envoya des détails au Duc de Sutherland: il envisageait de conduire les roues horizontales à partir de cylindres placès au dessus de la boite à fumée.**

<small>STAFFORDSHIRE RECORD OFFICE.</small>

compressing screw and bars for the horizontal wheels.

The solution was more, and more reliable, locomotives: a solution which a company with strained finances and limited life was ill placed to adopt. Fell had recommended additional engines as long before as March 1867, without success. However the Duke of Sutherland seems to have taken a personal interest in potential motive power. In May of that year the noted engineer John Fowler wrote to him approving calculations for design of goods engines and in March 1868 William Stroudley, then Locomotive Carriage & Wagon Superintendent of the Highland Railway, sent the duke details of a locomotive he had designed for the MCR.

In August 1868 the board grasped the nettle: T. R. Crampton went out to Mont Cenis to obtain Barnes's opinion on a proposed new type of engine. A. Alexander's appointment had terminated once the rolling stock was complete and by November he was working for Worcester Engine Works. The design of the new locomotives was undertaken by Crampton. The layout reverted to four cylinders, but the drive to the horizontal wheels was through gears; it is described further in chapter six. By mid-November, four locomotives were on order from Cail et Cie. Back in the 1850s, Cail had built Crampton Patent locomotives in quantity for the French main line companies. The Mont Cenis locomotives were to be hired on the deferred purchase principle, as the directors' report put it that December.

In March 1869 Fell took out a further patent (no. 889) covering fifteen detail improvements to central rail locomotives, carriages and permanent way.

Meanwhile, during autumn 1868, Longridge was running two passenger trains a day (one regular, one conditional on demand) each way over the whole line, and three goods trains each way between St Michel and Lanslebourg only, because of the lack of reliable motive power. 'Grande Vitesse' goods were carried throughout by rail, but 'Petite Vitesse' goods were carried between Lanslebourg and Susa by cart or sledge. Nevertheless, things were not as bad as they appeared to one critic who, noting an immense accumulation of goods at St Michel, assumed that the MCR was unable to carry it onward. Not so, wrote Longridge to The Times[45] in reply: it was goods which the MCR had brought from Italy, and which were detained at St Michel because the PLM had not repaired the breaches in its line.

In August, Bell had been urging the need to complete the covered ways. He was right but unheeded, for they were still incomplete when heavy snow fell unusually early in November. It started on the 7th and continued through the 8th and 9th until the morning of the 10th. The wind swept it into deep drifts and all personnel were employed under Longridge in keeping the line clear. Barnes wrote to Alexander[46] that the trains 'go through 1 metre [of snow] very respectably, but 6 metres thick is out of the question'.

As luck would have it, on the afternoon of 7 November one of the locomotives, hauling empty wagons, chose to break down three miles east of La Frontière and could not be moved until mid-day on the 8th. The passenger trains from St Michel were held overnight at La Frontière and La Grand' Croix at the height of the storm, and eventually reached Susa the following afternoon. On 8 November, the trains from St Michel were delayed to the same extent, purely by the snow. Meanwhile, on the evening of the 8th, when the trains which had left St Michel on the 7th had arrived at Susa, one of them attempted the return trip. Near Bard it stuck fast in a deep drift, and when eventually extracted was obliged to return to Susa. But in this period of exceptional weather, it was the only train to be cancelled,

and despite alarmist rumours which reached the press, there was no day when the railway was completely blocked. It was shortly after these events that Lord Mayo made his record-breaking passage of the railway.

It may have been at this time that Blount spent a week at the col. In his memoirs he recalled that the line was kept open despite 24 feet of snow. For companions he had driver Morton and his wife; for food they got excellent fish from the lake.

In March 1869 a train was isolated by enormous snow drifts which accumulated in front of it and behind. The mails were sent forward by sledge, which in turn was overwhelmed by an avalanche: the driver fortunately escaped but it took two days to dig out the letters.

Despite all the problems, the railway was proving profitable to operate. The operating accounts for the period from 15 June 1868 to 31 October were produced in December for presentation at a general meeting in February 1869: they are in francs, but it is evident that expenses represented only 73.44 per cent of receipts. During that period, too, traffic was still building up. But because of the borrowing needed to complete the line, the company was heavily in debt. The Mont Cenis balance sheet at 31 October 1868 showed £153,550 raised from issue of shares, but £180,750 from debentures and £17,500 from loans, with creditors of £65,486 7s 2d. Creditors in France had agreed to have part of their payment deferred, secured against the operating profit. This prevented payment of interest on bonds and shares. (Readers who are shareholders in Eurotunnel are probably reflecting that nothing much changes!)

The Duke of Sutherland took advantage of the upturn in the company's affairs to retire from the board. One senses Loch's influence; by now it must have been clear that the company could never fulfil its early promises, and it may well have been seen as impolitic for so immensely wealthy an individual to remain at the head of a concern in which ordinary shareholders were likely to lose their money. The duke also had increasing railway preoccupations nearer home: the Sutherland

*Ferrovia Fell - Moncenisio 1868-1872*

*Passengers have descended from a train at La Grand' Croix station while the locomotive takes water. To judge from the rolling stock it is probably a first class and mail train.*

**Des passagers descendent d'un train à la gare de Grand'Croix pendent qu'on alimente la locomotive en eau. A en juger par le matériel roulant, il s'agit probablement d'un train postal et de première classe.**
MUSÉES D'ART ET D'HISTOIRE DE CHAMBÉRY.

Railway, of which he was chairman, had opened from Bonar Bridge as far as Golspie in April 1868, but had then run out of funds - a problem which the duke was to solve by building the next section northwards at his own expense as the Duke of Sutherland's Railway. He retained a personal interest in the Mont Cenis - Cutbill was asked to send him a progress report in October 1869 - and he seconded adoption of the directors' report at the annual general meeting in February 1870.

Jervoise Smith had also retired from the board - it was his place which Longridge had taken. The directors of the company at the beginning of 1869, then, were Lord Abinger, Duke of Vallombrosa, Brassey, Dallas, Blount, Buddicom, Brogden, Fell and Longridge, with Abinger as Chairman. Brunlees subsequently joined the board, and the Duke of Vallombrosa left.

Brassey continued to take a close interest in the line. He certainly lent the company money from time to time: Cutbill, writing to the duke, mentioned financial problems in July 1869 (the French creditors were getting restless) and said that Brassey had come to the rescue again. It is intriguing to speculate on Brassey's continuing support for the railway even after the likelihood of making a direct profit from it had gone. If he retained a financial interest in the railways he had built in Italy, he could have profited indirectly from the traffic which the Mont Cenis fed to them - but I have been unable to establish whether he did in fact retain any such interest. The MCR was however regarded very much as an experimental line, a proving ground for the central rail system, so he may well have hoped to profit from contracts to build future central rail railways elsewhere. I am inclined to think too that he would have wished to avoid the bad publicity, from the point of view of obtaining future contracts for railways of any sort, which would result from failure of an undertaking with which he was so closely associated; and that he took a natural pride in completing a job once started.

Traffic in 1869 continued to improve. We know this, because from the opening until the end of 1870 the receipts were recorded in *The Times* on a weekly basis, with sufficient regularity to enable the graph which appears on page 53 to be prepared. The receipts must be closely related to the level of traffic, and the devastating effect of the floods of 1868 can be seen, as can the traffic peaks in spring and autumn, the most popular times for visits to Italy.

Among the many passengers who came in 1869 was Edward Whymper, who had originally been dispatched to the Alps in 1860 by publisher William Longman to produce illustrations for a book on the subject. Whymper was a skilled engraver, and a determined young man. Applying that determination to the ascent of unclimbed peaks, he became in 1865, after seven unsuccessful attempts, one of the party which was first to reach the summit of the Matterhorn. His descriptions of the Mont Cenis pass and its railway, which appeared in his own book *Scrambles amongst the Alps...* have already been mentioned. They are of particular interest because unlike most they date not from the opening of the railway but from a time when it had become fully established.

The Indian Mail was first carried over the Mont Cenis Railway on 15 October 1869. Presented with mail which arrived at Susa from Brindisi 67 minutes late, the MCR then recovered 57 minutes of the delay during the

*A mixed train halts at La Grand' Croix. What, one wonders, is under those tarpaulins: tunnelling machinery? Today this location is submerged by the hydro-electric reservoir.*
**Un train mixte fait halte à la Grand'Croix. Que trouverait-on sous ces bâches? des machines à creuser de tunnels? Aujourd'hui, ce site est submergé par le réservoir hydro-electrique.**
Musées d'Art et d'Histoire de Chambéry.

transit over its line. Initially a trial, the Indian Mail soon became a regular feature.

In general, the average speeds of trains were, between St Michel and Lanslebourg, 13.2 mph in both directions; between Lanslebourg and La Frontière 7.9 mph upwards and 10.6 mph downwards; and between La Frontière and Susa 10.6 mph downwards and 8.6 mph upwards.

Winter came early again in 1869. There was heavy snow in November, and again at the end of December when the line did become blocked and traffic was moved by sledges for some days. Snow was a perpetual problem; the covered ways were not wholly satisfactory, as the snow drifted inside them. One winter La Grand' Croix station was completely covered over, so that it was possible to walk over the top of it. Far down the sides of the pass the snow was often too deep for a plough to clear, and it had to be dug away by gangs of workmen.

However the winter of 1869 brought not only snow but also, at last, the Cail locomotives. They had been due in July: the first two arrived towards the end of November. They worked well and went straight into service during severe weather. With them the railway had a large enough stock of locomotives to work freight trains throughout. One important traffic was coal and materials consigned to Bardonèccia for use in construction of the tunnel. All the boring machinery used in the tunnel came from Cockerill of Seraing, Belgium. The heaviest train taken over the line was said to weigh 36 tons.

Development of goods traffic was hampered by the delays and cost of transhipment at St Michel and Susa. Brunlees later said that each ton of goods cost 8d in transhipment, with a day's delay[47]. Nevertheless carrying goods throughout by rail must have been a welcome relief to the directors, for carrying by cart or sledge cost almost as much as the charges made. In their report to the annual general meeting on 10 February 1870 they were still unable to promise, during the ensuing year, payment of interest to holders of bonds or shares. Traffic had not equalled expectations, though it was steadily improving.

Throughout the entire life of the railway, no passengers met with any accident - a remarkable achievement for a line at first regarded with so much trepidation. There were, regrettably, accidents involving employees. In December 1869 there was a serious derailment to a freight train between Susa and the summit; accounts[48] vary as to the precise circumstances, but agree that two of the train crew were killed. In 1868 an employee was thrown from a train when departing from Susa, and killed. A curious accident, apparently without injury, was a fire on board a train in 1868: it was found to have been caused by spontaneous ignition of a lot of matches sent among other goods and not declared.

J. B. Fell himself summed up the results of operation of the MCR when he addressed the British Association at its meeting in Liverpool in September 1870. During two years and three months' working, he said, trains had run more than 200,000 miles and had carried over 100,000 passengers in safety, as well as a considerable amount of merchandise. The Indian Mails had been carried without any delays to cause missed connections, and on one occasion when mail was received late from Brindisi, one hour and a quarter of lost time were made up in crossing Mont Cenis. (How one would like to have seen, and heard, that train pounding up to the summit, or reeling round the curves by Fort L'Essaillon!) By the route which the MCR established, delivery of the Indian Mails in London had been accelerated by 30 hours, and one night's travelling had been cut from the journey between Paris and Turin.

The Mont Cenis Railway had proved the mechanical practicability and the safety of the centre rail system.

# CHAPTER FIVE
# THE COMPLETION OF THE TUNNEL

Use of compressed-air machinery in boring the Mont Cenis Tunnel had been supplemented by use of dynamite, patented by Alfred Nobel in 1867. Early in 1870 it was stated that a total of 10,598 metres been bored, out of the total length of 12,220 metres. When Fell gave his paper to the British Association in September 1870 he was able to predict, accurately as it turned out, that it would be completed before the end of the following year. He was already looking further afield than Mont Cenis: the main thrust of his paper was not to report on the Mont Cenis Railway, but to promote use of the central rail system elsewhere.

In Brazil, the Cantagallo Railway was already under construction. To climb over a mountain range it would include 10 miles of incline (later said to be 7¼ miles), most of it at 1 in 13 and equipped with the central rail; curves would be from 40 to 100 metres radius (2 to 5 chains approximately), the gauge would again be 1.1 m, and above all it would be permanent. Locomotives were already being designed. Central rail railways were also proposed in India, Switzerland, Spain, and elsewhere in Italy and France.

In these circumstances the Mont Cenis Railway entered a sort of twilight period. The company was the subject of a petition to wind it up as early as July 1870, and J. A. Longridge was appointed provisional official liquidator. The railway continued to run, initially as busy as ever. But the Franco-Prussian War had broken out at the end of June, to be followed by revolution in France on 4 September. By the end of that month Paris was under siege. Blount remained in Paris: the senior member of the British community, he was appointed British consul in the absence of the ambassador, who had been instructed to withdraw along with the French government. For his efforts on behalf of Britons who stayed

in Paris through the siege and the famine which accompanied it he was eventually knighted.

The Mont Cenis Railway lay far from the battlefields and seems initially to have been little affected by the war. But the siege of Paris was another matter. The railway was largely dependent on long-distance traffic which passed through that city: and, at what should have been the busiest time of year, traffic fell to half or one third of its usual level. It was the end of January 1871 before there was an armistice, and travel via Paris eventually became possible again.

Thomas Brassey died on 8 December 1870 of bronchitis, aged sixty five. He was still in harness: one of his last contracts, for docks at Callao, had to be carried out by his executors.

After the end of 1870, the MCR traffic receipts were no longer reported in *The Times*, and the railway was omitted from the 1871 edition of *Bradshaw's Railway Manual*.

During the early 1870s the MCR was not the only central-rail railway to climb out of Lanslebourg towards the col. The Italian T. Agudio built a steeply-inclined line for trials of his system of cable traction. An endless cable ran upwards on one side of the track and down on the other: it was led round pulleys on the vehicle which were connected by gears and rods to wheels both horizontal and vertical. The effect was to reduce cable tension significantly, compared with a normal cable-worked incline. Agudio had earlier proposed, unsuccessfully, that his system should be used over part of the Mont Cenis Railway itself.

The tunnel breakthrough came on Christmas Day 1870, when tunnellers working from each end met. By early 1871 the Mont Cenis Railway was operating at a loss and, according to Pieri in *La Ferrovia del Moncenisio*, the company applied unsuccessfully to the Italian government for a subsidy; it then proposed premature closure of the line, but was obliged by the terms of its concession to continue to operate it.

Many months more were required to complete the tunnel but, despite concerns about ventilation, opening was eventually announced for 16 September. Those travelling out to Turin via France for the opening ceremonies were deposited by the PLM at St Michel on 15 September 1½ hours late, half an hour after the Mont Cenis train for Susa should have left. But on the MCR, where a deterioration in the service would not have been surprising, staff morale evidently remained good: the connection had been held, several trains were assembled and Turin passengers put on the first, which then made up eight minutes on the run to Susa despite being unusually heavy and running by night. Eventual arrival at Turin was at 2 am, with the inaugural train back scheduled to depart at 6.20[49].

The Mont Cenis Tunnel was indeed opened on 16 September, when a special train carrying 700 persons diverged from the Susa line at Bussoleno and passed through the tunnel in twenty two minutes, without asphyxiating its passengers, to reach Modane. There it terminated, returned to Bardonècchia for the celebratory banquet and eventually to Turin.

The tunnel was now complete, although with a single track only for the time being, but it was not opened to traffic. The PLM running true to form had failed to complete the 10-mile approach line - admittedly a difficult one to build - from St Michel to Modane. The Mont Cenis Railway's concessions still held and it continued to operate. Passengers who had travelled twice through the tunnel at its opening ceremony returned to France over the hill by the Fell railway.

It was not until 16 October 1871 that the through route was completed and opened to traffic. The last trains on the Mont Cenis Railway ran the previous day.

In speaking of this, J. A. Longridge[50] added that the train-miles run since 15 November 1868 amounted to 345,520, during which time the working expenses averaged 9s

8½d per train-mile of which locomotive expenses absorbed 4s 0d; the receipts per train-mile averaged 11s 9½d. The Fell system was, he concluded, a mechanical success, but expensive.

The Mont Cenis Tunnel as completed was 14,051 yards 2 feet long from portal to portal (curved approaches had been driven at each end leading into the main bore): that is to say, 85 feet short of 8 miles[51]. It had taken more than 14 years to make it. Despite continuing complaints of difficulties experienced by travellers on the PLM line serving it, the tunnel became and remains a vital component of the European rail network. It was a colossal achievement.

Yet to the passenger all that achievement meant was a twenty-minute trundle through the dark. The achievement of the Fell railway by contrast, as it hoisted its passengers up to the col and lowered them down the other side, was heroic, even sublime. As long before as 1866 *The Illustrated London News*[52] had suggested that people would prefer this route to the tunnel, and regular travellers regretted its closure. The company is said to have offered its equipment to the communes of Haut-Maurienne[53]. But the day had yet to dawn when every village in France, seemingly, would be linked to the main line by a roadside light railway. The offer was not taken up. The railway was dismantled.

Much equipment went to the Cantagallo Railway. Because its use there was eventually much less long-lived than Fell had hoped - as will be mentioned in the last chapter - it is difficult at this distance of time to be precise about what went to that far away location. However it appears to have included a substantial quantity of rails, and probably most or all of the locomotives except nos. 1 and 2. Staff probably went as well. In 1872, when one of the Fell locomotives built by Manning Wardle for the Cantagallo Railway was tried out in England before despatch, the driver once again was Thomas Morton. Latterly Assistant Superintendent on the Mont Cenis, he was planning to go out as Locomotive Superintendent on the Cantagallo where he was to have the assistance of another former

Mont Cenis driver, Henry Mason[54].

With the Lausanne-Echallens Railway we are on much surer ground. The concession was granted in the summer of 1872; the LE was built to 1 metre gauge, the first narrow gauge public railway in Switzerland. Permanent way materials, locomotives and rolling stock were all obtained from Mont Cenis, and the line, ten miles long, was opened in stages in 1873 and 1874. The locomotives were nos. 1 and 2, and with them went twelve coaches, five fourgons, one goods van, fourteen open wagons and six flat wagons. Of these, four of the coaches and two of the fourgons were six-wheelers. All of these were modified to suit the narrower gauge and, since the ruling gradient on the LE was 1 in 25, the centre rail wheels and gear were removed.

Locomotives nos. 1 and 2 were named *Lausanne* and *Echallens* respectively and appear to have worked all traffic over the line for some months. But the company was also able to obtain two new 0-4-0Ts from Schneider & Cie, at an advantageous price because they were ordered at the same time as similar locomotives for a contractor building the Gotthard Line. These two locomotives proved preferable to those from the Mont Cenis. MCR no.1 was found to be heavy on fuel and difficult to maintain, and tended to damage the track. It was sold in 1874 to a Gotthard Line contractor. No. 2 was considered heavy and unstable, due to excessive overhang. In 1875 it was rebuilt, but in 1880 it too was sold. At that point we lose track of these two locomotives; regrettably, the LE does not seem to have found them a good bargain.

The careers of the carriages and wagons, by contrast, were as long as those of the locomotives were short. The Lausanne-Echallens Railway in due course absorbed a separate company which had extended the line and became the Lausanne-Echallens-Bercher Railway. In most countries such a railway would long since have been closed or amalgamated, but this is Switzerland: the LEB was electrified in 1935 and continues to operate under the same ownership.

All its former Mont Cenis carriages and wagons, although subject down the years to

*Many items of Mont Cenis rolling stock, after a short career on the line for which they were built, ran for many decades on the Lausanne-Echallens-Bercher Railway. One of the first class coaches is seen here as running in 1910.*

***Après avoir servi brièvement sur la ligne pour laquelle elles avaient été construites, plusieurs pieces du materiel roulant du Mont Cenis furent utilisées pendant de nombreuses décennies sur la ligne Lausanne-Echallens-Bercher. Une des voitures de première classe apparait ici en 1910.***

CREDIT: SEE ACKNOWLEDGEMENTS.

innumerable alterations, modifications and re-buildings, lasted in one form or another well into the present century. One of the coaches survived, un-rebuilt, until electrification and some of the goods stock lasted even longer, into the 1960s.

Meanwhile the underframes of some of the coaches, and some of the wagons, had been rebuilt to become flat-wagons: one of the sights of Lausanne, it seems, in the 1960s was a rake of these distinguished nonagenarians, fully loaded with milk churns, in tow behind a modern electric motor coach. In 1981 the LEB, conscious of its heritage, took the chassis from one of these wagons and mounted upon it a coach body which it had been able to recover, to produce the Mont Cenis coach for the steam specials which it had introduced.

Other equipment, too, had been purchased by the Lausanne-Echallens from the Mont Cenis. In 1965 the then director of the LEB made a gift to an enthusiast friend of an ancient oil lamp from the company's station at Lausanne. It was only when thick layers of old paint were removed that an oval plate was revealed reading 'CHEMIN DE FER DU MONT-CENIS'.

There are persistent stories, all from secondary sources which I have been unable to confirm, that some of the Mont Cenis stock went to Argentina, either direct or else via the Rigi. It is perhaps significant that J. A. Longridge did visit Argentina, in connection with railway construction, in 1875. Pieri states that rails seem to have been offered to the Rigi Railway, but that the sale was not concluded and that they went to a mineral railway in Tuscany instead.

The limited records of the Mont Cenis Railway Company which survive in the Public Record Office do not reveal how the proceeds of these sales were distributed among the creditors, or whether there was anything left for the shareholders. Indeed Longridge appears not to have concluded his tasks as liquidator. He retired from business in 1881 and moved to Jersey where he died in 1896. The Companies Registration Office had written to him in 1891 requesting accounts, probably without tracing him and evidently without receiving any. In January 1902 the Companies Office wrote to him again, at his former business address, and not unnaturally received no reply. Three months later The Mont Cenis Railway Company (Limited) was compulsorily dissolved.

*LEB flat wagon, carrying milk churns in 1951, was built on the underframe of a Mont Cenis coach.*
**Ce wagon plat LEB, transportant des bidons de lait en 1951, fut construit sur le chassis d'un wagon du Mont Cenis.**
H. U. WURSTEN SEE ACKNOWLEDGMENTS.

# CHAPTER SIX
# LOCOMOTIVES &
# ROLLING STOCK

Because development of Mont Cenis Railway locomotives and rolling stock was so closely interwoven with progress of the whole project, much has already been written here about them. However it is now worth adding some further details which, if given before, would have interrupted the historical narrative too much.

## LOCOMOTIVES

No. 1. 0-4-0ST, built Brassey Jackson Betts & Co. 1863[55].

The boiler was 7 feet 9$^{1}/_{2}$ inches long by 2 feet 9 inches diameter. There were 100 tubes of 1$^{1}/_{2}$ inches outside diameter. The total heating surface was 420 sq. feet, the grate area about 6 feet. The maximum working pressure was 120 lb/sq. inch. Mounted above the firebox to feed the boiler was a Giffard injector, invented only in 1859. The weight of the locomotive, including fuel (coke) and water, was 16 to 17 tons.

The two outside cylinders were 11$^{1}/_{4}$ inches diameter by 1 foot 6 inches stroke; they drove the vertical wheels, which were 2 feet 3 inches diameter, with a wheelbase of 5 feet 3 inches The positions of the inside cylinders, and the layout of the drive from them to the horizontal wheels, can be seen in the illustrations on pages 19 and 66. The extremely cramped location meant that the connecting rods for the horizontal wheels were very short, and worked at too great an angle: rotation of these wheels was irregular.

The dimensions of the inside cylinders were 11 inches diameter by 10 inches stroke; the horizontal wheels were 16 inches diameter with a wheelbase of 1 feet 7 inches Each was mounted on a vertical axle with upper and lower axleboxes; these were allowed some horizontal movement, towards and away from the centre rail, and linked together so as to move in unison. Pressure on the centre rail was provided by a combination of strong volute springs - two to each lower axlebox - and cams, operated through gearing from a hand wheel, which worked in small frames attached to each axlebox and so separated opposing boxes or brought them closer together. The maximum load on the centre rail was 12 tons; at Whaley Bridge a load of 8 tons only was used. For the Lanslebourg trials, the maximum was increased to 16 tons. There were two regulators and two reversing levers, one for each set of cylinders and wheels.

Desbrière stated that there were two sorts of brakes. There was a brake acting on the central rail - its two shoes clasped that rail between them - but it had been positioned so close to one of the extremities of the locomotive (the drawing which appears on page 66 shows it beneath the footplate) that it could only be used on straight track. On curves, brakes with wooden blocks bearing on the rear vertical wheels had to be used. There is no sign of these on the drawing, which suggests they were added when the need for them emerged during the earliest trials. Tyler, who saw the locomotive only at Lanslebourg, stated that guide wheels had 'been added to the trailing end of the engine to act on the middle rail'[56]. They may have replaced the sledge brakes, for there would have been little room for them otherwise. Alexander claimed that difficulties likely to arise from the 'quick curves' of the MCR were not drawn to his attention until some months after the locomotive had been at work in Derbyshire[57]. No.1 had the reputation of being always short of steam, evidently due in part to the demands of four cylinders.

No. 2. 0-4-0T built James Cross & Co. 1864-5, builder's no. 2[58].

In designing this locomotive the

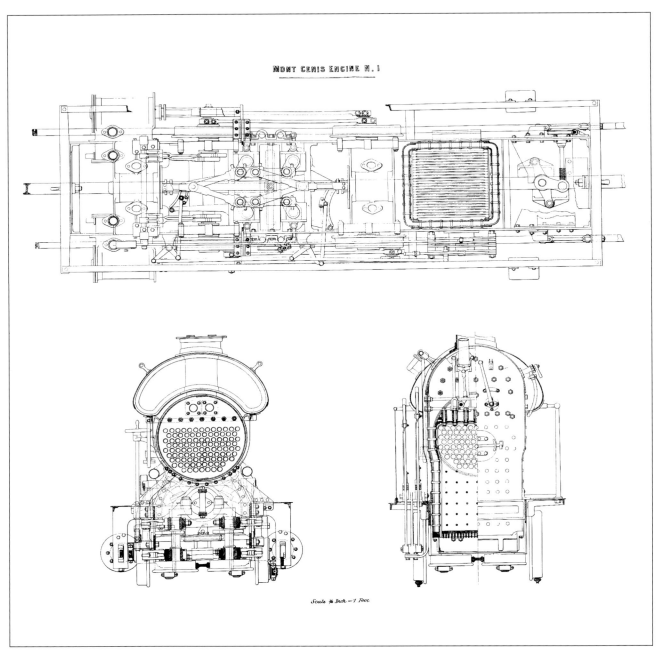

MONT CENIS ENGINE N. 1

Scale ¾ Inch = 1 Foot

opportunity was taken not only to simplify the drive mechanism, but also, since it was perceived that most of the adhesion would come from the central rail, to reduce the weight - or, rather, to produce a more powerful locomotive without increasing the weight. To that end boiler shell, wheels, axles and parts of the motion were made of steel. This was pioneering stuff, for use of steel as a

boiler material had yet to emerge from the experimental stage.

The boiler was enlarged, compared with no. 1, to be 8 feet 4½ inches long and 3 feet 2 inches in diameter, and the number of tubes was increased to 158, still of 1½ inches external diameter. The total heating surface became 600 sq. feet, and the grate area 10 sq. feet. The maximum working pressure was 120 lb/sq. inch The two cylinders were 15 inches diameter by 16 inches stroke; all wheels were 2 feet 3 inches diameter. The frames, rather unusually for the period, were outside the wheels, no doubt to increase the space available for the central rail drive. The wheelbase of the vertical wheels was 6 feet 10 inches, and of the horizontal wheels, 2 feet 4 inches The weight in working order, as built, remained at 16-17 tons for a locomotive said to be 50 per cent more powerful than no. 1. Experience soon showed, however, that the pursuit of lightness had been overdone: some parts connected with the drive to the vertical wheels were insufficiently robust and had to be replaced by others which were heavier, to a total extent of some 4 cwt.

Cross's drawing reproduced on page 26 shows that the crown of the firebox was lower towards the rear that at the front. I have nowhere seen this feature commented upon, but it seems reasonable to infer that it was intended to prevent the rear of the crown from becoming uncovered by water when the locomotive was heading down the 1 in 12.

There was no link motion and the valves were actuated, and the locomotive reversed, by means of shifting eccentrics on the front axle[59]. The means by which both the horizontal wheels and the vertical wheels were driven has been described in chapter two.

The means of applying pressure to the central rail was improved too. On each side of the locomotive, the axleboxes of the vertical axles were mounted on lengthways cradles which were allowed crosswise movement. Pressing these inward on either side was a row of six volute springs. Bearing on the outer side of each row of springs were two bars; through the centres of these passed a crosswise shaft, threaded left- and right-handed and engaging with holes threaded likewise in the bars. This shaft was mounted between the frames of the locomotive and could be turned, through gears, by a handwheel mounted on the footplate to alter the pressure on the central rail. The maximum pressure was 24 tons; a pressure of 12 tons was used during the Lanslebourg trials.

The layout of the brakes is something of a mystery for, like some other features of the locomotive, they are not shown fully on Cross's drawing. Fell wrote in 1866[60] 'The brakes are applied to the outside wheels, but act upon the inside ones; also through the medium of the connecting and piston rods'. The semi-colon appears to be an intrusion inserted perhaps by editor or type setter. Fell added that there were also brakes to grip the central rail.

The overhang forward of the front axle was 6 feet 2 inches and to the rear of the rear axle as much as 7 feet 10 in; so there was a load of about 6 tons on the front axle and 11 tons on the rear. When running at 12 to 15 mph the locomotive pitched badly and, where there was no central rail, was inclined to derail. Presumably it was this experience that led to the decision to design the Gouin locomotives as 0-4-2Ts.

Nos. 3-5, 0-4-2Ts built Emile Gouin et Cie, 1866-7, builder's nos. 673-675
Nos. 6-14, 0-4-0Ts built Emile Gouin et Cie, 1867-8, builder's nos. 676-688

The early reconstruction of the first three locomotives as 0-4-0Ts has been mentioned in chapter three. The principal source of detailed information about these twelve locomotives is the condensed specification which appeared in *The Engineer*[61]. This, signed by Abinger and Brogden, was in essence the specification to which Gouin was to build: but it was published as a description of them after they were all complete. All reference to the trailing wheels has, it was admitted, been edited out; the accompanying drawing of an elevation, reproduced as an illustration on page 68, has a conspicuous blank space below the cab! It seems reasonable to suppose, therefore, that it was updated in any other essentials where necessary. An earlier description was published in *Engineering* for 29 March 1867: that is to say, while the locomotives were still being built so that it appears to describe, to some extent, intentions rather than actualities.

A. Alexander forwarded detailed drawings to France and supervised construction. Once again there was much use of steel: for, among other things, the plates of the boiler and the

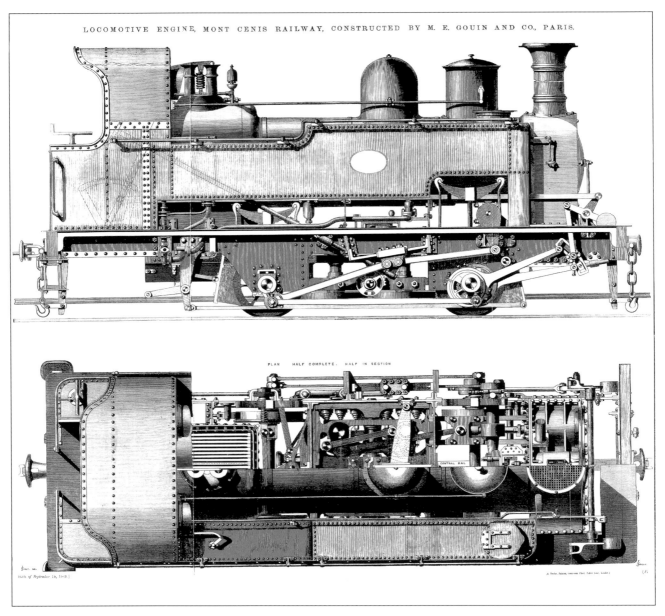

LOCOMOTIVE ENGINE, MONT CENIS RAILWAY, CONSTRUCTED BY M. E. GOUIN AND CO, PARIS.

PLAN HALF COMPLETE. HALF IN SECTION

*The Gouin locomotives in their eventual form were described in detail to readers of The Engineer on 18 September 1868.*
***Les locomotives Gouin dans leur forme éventuelle furent décrites en détail aux lecteurs de 'The Engineer' le 18 septenbre 1868.***

outer firebox, the front tubeplate, the main frames and the connecting rods. The boiler, enlarged again by comparison with no. 2, was about 9 feet 6 inches long and about 3 feet 7 inches diameter. The heating surface was increased, to 850 sq. feet. The boiler barrel sloped slightly downwards towards the front, so that the front ends of the tubes were 2 inches lower than the rear: provision for maintaining the correct water level when facing up the 1 in 12. The rear of the firebox

crown was also lowered as on no. 2, but (unlike no. 2) the outer firebox rose substantially higher than the boiler barrel. The boiler was fed by a pump and an injector.

The cylinders were 1 feet 4 inches diameter by 1 feet 4 inches stroke, though no. 14 was said to have cylinders 1 feet 3 inches diameter[62]. A pipe, with a tap which could be worked from the footplate, led from the front tubeplate to the blastpipe: this enabled boiler water, in the form of a spray of water and steam, to be fed into the steam chest to lubricate valves and pistons when the locomotive was running forwards downhill but in back gear for braking.

All wheels were 2 feet 4 inches diameter. The wheelbase of the vertical wheels was 7 feet 6 inches[63] and that of the horizontal wheels about 2 feet 6 inches There were heavy balance weights on the vertical wheels, to increase the steadiness of the engine. Pressure was applied to the central rail by a means similar to that of no. 2; the threaded adjusting shaft was made of steel. There were brake blocks bearing on all four vertical wheels, and a clasp brake on the central rail located just ahead of the rear axle.

On each side of the footplate was a coal bunker and ahead of it a water tank. Sanding was by steam jet. There were rail guards for all three rails, fitted with sockets for a snow plough. The top of the chimney was fitted with a wire mesh spark catcher.

Despite attempts to keep the weight down, the overall weight in working order was 21 to 22 tons. The builder had insisted on being paid according to weight of materials used.

Like no. 2, these locomotives rode badly. Whymper, who was evidently given a footplate ride, wrote of the descent towards Susa: 'The engine vibrates, oscillates, and bounds; it is a matter of difficulty to hold on....An ordinary engine, moving at fifty miles an hour, with a train behind it, is not usually very steady, but its motion is a trifle compared with that of a Fell engine when running down hill'.

The bad riding of these locomotives seems likely to have been partly due to design faults about which little was said initially, though Fell was later more forthcoming. To the British Association[64] he said in 1870: 'The outside connecting rods between the rocking shafts and vertical driving wheels are placed at an angle to the cylinders, and the horizontal distance between the crank pins and the piston rod is slightly increased and diminished at the moment of passing the dead points when the engine rises and falls in the springs. As a corresponding movement cannot take place in the connecting rods of the inside gearing, a portion of the weight of the engine is thrown

upon them and on the cranks, causing an increase of wear and tear, loss of power, and occasional break-downs of the engines'.

Later still, in 1889, he told the Institution of Civil Engineers[65]: '...there was the difficulty that the outside wheels were worked by rocking-shafts and by oblique connecting-rods; and, although the diameter of the inside and outside wheels was exactly the same, they did not travel at the same rate at the same time. For instance, each quarter of a revolution was made in less time by one set of wheels than by the other, and there was a scrub, which caused a great deal of friction, wear and tear, and sometimes breakages'.

Alexander elsewhere showed expertise in layout of linkages - the arrangements for coupling the horizontal wheels across the locomotive were very neat - and can scarcely have been unaware of the imperfections in the layout of the drive to the vertical wheels; this had, too, been passed by the engineers on the board. It seems more likely that they underestimated the effects, and thought they would be acceptable in preference to the still more complicated layout needed to eliminate them.

Bad materials, therefore, were not the sole cause of breakages to the rocking shafts and the offset cranks, though no doubt they contributed to them, and to breakages of the compressing screws. The water tanks also gave trouble, from bad working practice: plates and angle irons had been rivetted together with paper for a jointing material, and burst joints were common. Alexander had objected to this practice when the locomotives were being built, to no avail: the builder's men were 'unaccustomed to do otherwise'[66]. Repairs to these locomotives involved the company in heavy and unwelcome expense.

Locomotive Superintendent Barnes attempted to design an improved means of coupling the two sets of horizontal wheels. Incorporating gears, it was fitted to locomotive no. 9, without success. He was successful, however, in fitting a rubber tube to an injector, to direct steam at the icebound motion of locomotives extracted from snowdrifts and so to thaw it out.

Nos. 15 - 18, 0-4-0Ts built Cail et Cie, 1868-9, builder's nos. 1742-1745

Crampton designed these with four cylinders and separate drive to vertical and horizontal wheels. The decision to do so no doubt harked back to Fell's earlier and unfulfilled wish to have such locomotives. The four cylinders[67] were in line across the locomotive; all four were 330 mm (1 feet 1 inch) diameter by 460 mm (1 feet 6$^1$/$_8$ inches) stroke. The outside cylinders drove the vertical wheels, which were 850mm (2 feet 9$^7$/$_{16}$ inches) diameter, the inside ones the horizontal wheels of 500 mm (1 feet 7$^{11}$/$_{16}$ inches) diameter. There were two vertical crankshafts, each of which carried a single large-diameter pinion: this meshed not only with pinions on the shafts carrying the horizontal driving wheels on its side of the locomotive, but also with its opposite number on the other side to maintain the quartering. Leaf springs pressed the horizontal wheels against the central rail, the load being varied by means of a threaded shaft.

There were also two pairs of horizontal unpowered rollers of 250 mm (9$^{13}$/$_{16}$ inches) diameter, positioned front and rear and just over 8 feet apart to provide additional lateral guidance. Presumably they would have been needed if the locomotive was running downhill with the horizontal wheels stationary and disengaged from the central rail. The clasp brake was located, as on the Gouins, ahead of the rear axle.

The boiler diameter was 1120 mm (3 feet 8$^1$/$_8$ inches), the rear of the firebox crown was lower than the front; and the weight empty was 21 tons. The weight in working order was about 26 tons and the centre of gravity was high, which led to poor stability and a jerking motion.

In place of the steam sanding gear of the earlier locomotives, cakes of sand mixed with adhesive resin were used. These are variously said to have been applied, under pressure, to the rims of the horizontal wheels[68], or to the central rail directly[69]. Probably both methods were tried.

On 24 January 1870 V. G. Bell, who was by then described as Locomotive Superintendent[70], wrote to Brunlees that the engines were admirably constructed, and that the materials and workmanship were all that could be desired.

ROLLING STOCK

The numbering system for rolling stock used a prefix letter to indicate the type of carriage or wagon, followed by a numeral for the consecutive number of each vehicle of that type. The Lausanne-Echallens Railway perpetuated the system, although sooner or later all the vehicles were re-numbered[71]. MCR prefixes which are known, from carriages and wagons which went to the LE, are as follows:

| | |
|---|---|
| A | Four-wheeled 1st class carriage |
| B | Four-wheeled 2nd class carriage |
| C | Four-wheeled 3rd class carriage |
| D | Four-wheeled fourgon |
| AA | Six-wheeled 1st class carriage |
| BB | Six-wheeled 2nd class carriage |
| DD | Six-wheeled fourgon |
| K | Four-wheeled goods van |
| L | Four-wheeled open wagon |
| M | Four-wheeled flat wagon. |

Initially, carriages and wagons were fitted with two pairs of horizontal wheels, with flanges below the central rail. One pair of wheels was subsequently removed, to ease passage of sharp curves, and it seems likely that the flanges were also. When coaches were being ordered it was intended that on the four-wheelers some at least of the vertical wheels should run loose on their axles. I have found no mention of this feature in descriptions of rolling stock at the time of opening of the line, so it seems likely to have been omitted.

Early drawings of locomotives nos. 1 and 2 depict them fitted with side buffers. On the railway as completed centre buffer-couplings were used, link and pin couplings being incorporated into the buffers.

FOUR-WHEELED COACHES AND FOURGONS

There survives in the Metro-Cammell collection at Birmingham Central Library a drawing for 'Underframe for Tramway Carriage' described as 'Mr Fell's'. (I am indebted to Michael Messenger for drawing my attention to this.) The drawing is Metropolitan Railway Carriage & Wagon Co. no. 1036, dated 9 February 1865 and reproduced here on page 27. It shows a wooden underframe with wheels and running gear, and ironwork for an end balcony and steps. No brakes or horizontal wheels are shown, but this drawing seems likely to depict the underframe for the coach which Capt. Tyler found on the Lanslebourg experimental line, and which was later used for the triumphant first run over the whole length of the railway. The back-to-back dimension between the wheels is shown as 3 feet 3 inches (991mm), and length and width tally with those given by Tyler.

It appears that all the subsequent MCR carriages and wagons were built by Chevalier, Cheilus & Cie. The numbers of the four-wheeled coaches and fourgons eventually transfered to the Lausanne-Echallens Railway were A4, A5, A6; B2, B3; C2, C3, C6; D1, D3 and D4. From their numbers it is evident that the MCR had at least six 1st class four-wheelers, three 2nd class, six 3rd class, and four fourgons.

These vehicles were about 14 feet 9 inches long over the body, 6 feet 7 inches wide and 6 feet 10$^{3}/_{4}$ inches high. The wheels were 2 feet 3$^{1}/_{2}$ inches diameter, with a wheelbase of 6 feet 1 inches[72] Their seating arrangement, along the sides and facing inwards, was familiar from omnibuses and street tramways.

The first carriage, exhibited at the Paris international exhibition in May 1867[73], was first class and laid out with four compartments of which the middle two seated four passengers and the end ones two only. The carriage was lined in 'drab cloth' (i.e., light brown) up to about half its height; above this were windows, matching the compartments so

*In this Lausanne-Echallens train of the 1880s, everything behind the locomotive is of Mont Cenis origin. An M-series flat wagon is followed by LE fourgon no. D2, which had been converted from MCR goods van no. K2. The coach is a former six-wheeler with the middle pair of wheels removed, and is followed by another coach, unidentified. Probably the trackwork too is from Mont Cenis.*

***Dans ce train Lausanne-Echallens des années 1880, tout sauf la locomotive est originaire de Mont Cenis. Un wagon plat de série M est suivi d'un fourgon LE no. D2 qui était à l'origine un wagon couvert Mont Cenis no. K2. La voiture avait six roues dont la paire du milieu a été enlevée, et est suivie d'une autre voiture non identifiée. Les rails datent probablement aussi de Mont Cenis.***

CREDIT:
SEE ACKNOWLEDGEMENTS.

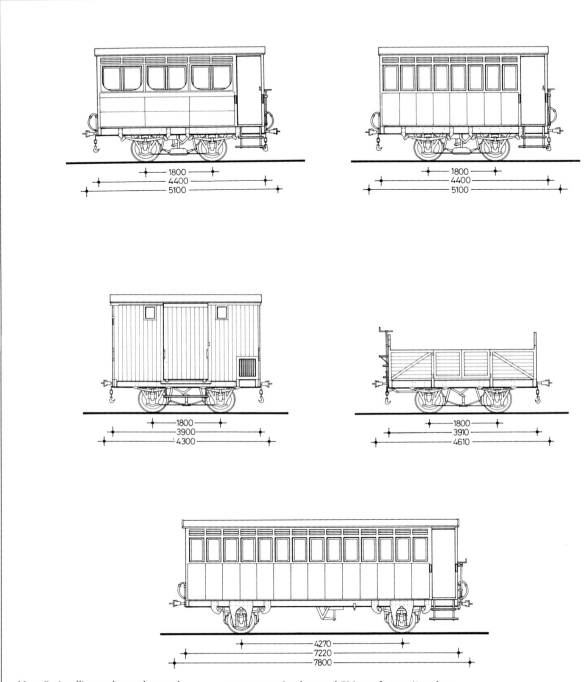

*Mont Cenis rolling stock, as subsequently operated on the Lausanne-Echallens Railway* **Le materiel roulant du Mont Cenis, utilisé ultérieurement pour le Chemin de Fer Lausanne-Echallens**

ABOVE LEFT, *1st class coach/***Voiture de première classe**
ABOVE RIGHT, *2nd/3rd class coach/***Voiture de deuxième/troisième classe**
CENTRE LEFT, *fourgon/***fourgon**
CENTRE RIGHT, *open wagon/***Wagon ouvert**
BELOW, *2nd class coach converted from six wheels to four/***Voiture de deuxième classe, reconstruite de six roues à quatre.**
CREDIT: SEE ACKNOWLEDGEMENTS.

that on each side there were two wide ones flanked by a narrow one each end. It is evident from photographs that the arrangement of compartments varied from one first class carriage to another.

One cause for complaint which reached a letter to the editor of *The Times*[74] - the class of carriage is not stated but seems likely to have been 1st - was that the hat pegs were placed above the windows and, since they were used for hanging rugs and shawls out of the way of their owners, they should be moved for the benefit of those who desired to see the scenery.

Second and third class carriages can be recognised in photographs from their rows of much smaller windows. The fourteen passengers in a second class carriage got upholstered seats and seat backs but no armrests; the sixteen passengers in a third class carriage had wooden seats only. It is the body of third class no. C6 which now forms part of the restored ex-MCR carriage on the LEB.

There are many contemporary references to the fourgons. Unfortunately although these note their existence, they say little of what they were actually like. They appear, however, as the leading vehicles in the trains illustrated on pages 54, 58 and 59. There they can be seen to have sides of matchboarding, a large sliding door, two small windows high up, and a dog box bottom right. The roof has railings round it so that, presumably, luggage can be stowed upon it. At one end is an elevated rectangular projection above the roof which might well be a guard's lookout.

## SIX-WHEELED COACHES AND FOURGONS

The six-wheelers eventually transfered to the Lausanne-Echallens Railway were nos. AA1, AA2, BB1, BB2, DD1 and DD2. Contemporary references to these vehicles on the MCR are few, so it may be that two of each type was the total roster. No. AA1 was fitted out as an observation saloon - one end had no communicating door, but was semi-circular and glazed.

All the six-wheelers, apparently, were built with Clark's radial axles: John Clark's system (patent no. 2328 of 1864) was one of several developed at this period to provide flexibility in six-wheeled vehicles. The middle axle was allowed side play. Each of its axle boxes was fitted with bell cranks for which the axle-guards provided the fulcra, and which were linked to the outer axles by thrust rods. The effect on a curve was that when the central axle moved sideways, the outer axles were pivoted to match the radius of the curve. These coaches were 23ft 8¼ inches over the body. Fell, as mentioned earlier, spoke well of the six-wheelers when addressing the British Association in 1870. He pointed out that there was less dead weight than with four-wheelers. Nevertheless, the Lausanne-Echallens Railway found maintenance of the flexible wheelbase excessively onerous: it removed the centre axles during 1875-6 and subsequently ran the vehicles as four-wheelers. One of the coaches, which looks like BB1 or BB2, appears in this form in the illustration on page 71.

## GOODS ROLLING STOCK

The goods rolling stock eventually transferred to the Lausanne-Echallens Railway comprised:

| | |
|---|---|
| Goods Van | K2 |
| Open Wagons | L1, L2, L3, L4, L5, L12, L15, L20, L25, L30, L36, L43, L45, L46 |
| Flat Wagons | M4, M5, M6, M8, M14, M16. |

From the numbering it is evident that, unless there were gaps in the series, the MCR had at least 64 goods vehicles, which is consistent with the totals quoted earlier of 103 or, alternatively, 95. Lower totals, such as 20 or 32, given in several recent publications seem clearly incorrect.

Goods vans appear as the second vehicles in the trains illustrated on pages 54 and 58. They can be seen to have sliding doors and what appear to be a series of openable vents along the side: these suggest they may have been designed to be available to carry livestock. The most conspicuous feature, however, is a brakesman's cabin which towers above the roof at one end. Considering these illustrations, and the MCR's limited stock of fourgons, it seems probable that when contemporary observers described trains as including two 'fourgons' - as on the opening day - that one of them may have been a goods van. The LE seems to have converted van K2 to match its other fourgons, with dog box and small windows, before putting it into service: in this guise it appears in the illustration on page 71.

Two open wagons described in *Engineering*[75] could each take a load of 5 tons. They each had one pair of horizontal guide wheels, and brakes acting on the central rail and on the vertical wheels. Elevated brakesman's cabins seem to have been a feature of the open wagons as of the vans. They were removed by the LE, to judge from photographs, from all the MCR rolling stock which it had acquired. Goods stock inherited by the LE ran on underframes similar to the four-wheeled passenger coaches, but had slightly shorter bodies. This enabled the LEB in 1981 to unite running gear which had originated beneath MCR flat wagon no. M16 (iron frames had replaced wood about 1913) with the body from coach no. C6 to provide the coach which runs in its steam specials. The wheelbase was lengthened for improved riding, which altered the appearance of the coach, but nonetheless it remains in essence a Mont Cenis vehicle.

## SNOWPLOUGH

In January 1867 Fell and Brunlees were authorised by the board to consult together about a snowplough and to spend not more than £200 on it. The snowplough was designed by Alexander on the basis of experience of dealing with snow in Canada. It was built on a four-wheeled wooden frame with additional horizontal guide wheels. The lower part scooped up snow from rail level - a slot had to be left for the central rail - and the upper part was movable, so that the snow could be discharged to left or right according to which side was road and which was precipice[76].

## OPERATION

How were these locomotives and rolling stock operated? To take locomotives nos.1 and 2 first[77], after the line was open no. 1 is said to have been used for shunting at St Michel, but to have been dismantled for some time prior to closure. No. 2 shunted at Susa and was used for works trains. It was claimed that it was not authorised to run on the French part of the line: this sounds as though it was kept to the Susa-Lanslebourg half of the line with its long sections equipped with the central rail.

The Cail locomotives generally operated between St Michel and Lanslebourg[78]. The harder part of the railway over the hill from Lanslebourg to Susa continued to be the preserve of the Gouins. For all their defects and unreliability, the Gouins steamed better than the Cails, for their exhaust was regular, and they traversed two-chain curves more easily. They also rode less roughly on the central rail than off it.

The Cail locomotives by contrast did not steam well. Their boilers were unable to supply sufficient steam for both sets of cylinders simultaneously, and the fault was aggravated by the irregular exhaust. This was a consequence of having two sets of cylinders and driving wheels running at different speeds. The Cail locomotives were better suited than the Gouins to sections - extensive between St Michel and Lanslebourg - where there was no central rail. They ran faster; when off the central rail, steam was shut off from the cylinders which drove the horizontal wheels, which saved on wear and tear.

A paradox arose over the pressure to be applied to the central rail. Brunlees, after carrying out trials with no. 2 on the Lanslebourg experimental line in 1865, foresaw no problem in increasing the pressure from the 12 tons used in the trials to the maximum designed pressure of 24 tons. At that period the thinking was that a Fell locomotive should be made as light as possible, and as much adhesion as possible derived from the central rail. On 8 June 1868, however, *Engineering*'s reporter found the driver of his train from Lanslebourg applying only 9 tons pressure upon the horizontal wheels to carry them to the summit.

In fact experience soon showed that placing too high a pressure on the central rail had substantial disadvantages. It overstressed the motion causing breakages which meant long and costly repairs; it increased the resistance on curves; and it entailed a shock when a locomotive ran on to or off the central rail, for drivers always applied the pressure to the wheels beforehand and released it afterwards.

So drivers tended to minimise the pressure applied to the central rail. But this meant that slipping, instead of being rare, became commonplace: and that in turn was known to damage the motion.

This leads to considering to what extent the line was worked without use of the central rail. In 1880 Longridge recalled that 'for months he worked the line without a central rail, simply with the ordinary wheels. The central rail gear was broken down; for months the line was worked without it, and he regularly took up trains of 21 tons, and sometimes of 24 tons'.[79] This is a tantalisingly imprecise statement. What it appears to say is that throughout the whole line, and on every locomotive, the central rail and the associated drive mechanism were unusable: but that can scarcely have been the case. What is more likely is that certain sections were regularly operated without using the central rail, and that certain locomotives were operated by

adhesion alone when the drive to their horizontal wheels was damaged.

Here is Whymper's description of departure eastbound from Modane:

> ...there is one of the steepest inclines on the line, and it seems preposterous to suppose that any train could ascend it. A stoppage of ten minutes is made at Modane, and on leaving that station, the train goes off at the hill with a rush. In a few yards its pace is reduced, and it comes down and down to about four miles an hour, which speed is usually maintained until the incline is passed...

Despite the steepness of the incline, this does not sound much like a Fell engine clambering up the central rail, but much more like a driver stopping to build up a full head of steam and then taking a run at the bank, relying on adhesion alone. Indeed we know that the Modane incline was sometimes worked by adhesion alone, at least in dry weather, for other sources confirm that it was so[80] and indeed suggest that other steep inclines were on occasion worked likewise.

The central rail was in any event of great value for braking. Going downhill, locomotives were usually braked by being run in mid- or reverse gear, but the central rail brakes on the coaches and wagons were used with great skill by the brakesmen to keep the train under control.

# CHAPTER SEVEN
# THE AFTERMATH

Long before closure of the Mont Cenis Railway, Fell was already looking to the Cantagallo Railway for the continued development of the central rail system, and elimination of its problems.

In his 1870 paper to the British Association he described the layout of locomotives to be built for it, improving on the geared drive of the Cail locomotives. The cylinders for the horizontal wheels were to be one above the other on the centre line of the locomotive, and each was to drive, through rods, the horizontal wheels on both sides of it. This neatly maintained the quartering of the horizontal wheels while eliminating the gears and simplifying the drive. The detailed design work was done by Manning, Wardle & Co. who built three locomotives, 0-4-0Ts, in 1872[81]. The first was tried out on a line laid on the disused Goathland incline of the Whitby & Pickering Railway (the present-day North Yorkshire Moors Railway uses the deviation line which had been built to avoid the inclined plane).

The Fell incline of the Cantagallo Railway, inland from Rio de Janeiro, rose from 728 feet above sea level to 3,542 feet over 7.64 miles; the maximum gradient was 1 in 11 and the sharpest curve 1.4 chains. These figures were given in 1935 by the railway's then resident engineer[82] and, though different from Fell's 1870 figures quoted in chapter five, seem likely to be correct for the railway as built.

The sharpness of the curves is remarkable, for in 1871 it was written of the 2-chain curves of the Mont Cenis Railway that 'they have made sad work with the engines, particularly with their mid-motions or horizontal driving wheels ... and the centre rail itself, in consequence of excessive friction ... has been rolled out and reduced in dimensions so that the guide wheels of the carriages and the horizontal driving wheels of the engines cannot work over it in the smooth and easy manner that they did at the commencement...'.[83]

Unfortunately this feature proved to be the undoing of the Cantagallo incline. On the locomotives the drive mechanism for the horizontal wheels was found to be mounted too rigidly in the frames for it to follow irregularities in the middle rail. Fractures became frequent. In 1883 powerful conventional 0-6-0Ts from Baldwin, without flanges on the centre pair of wheels, were introduced. They proved able to haul up the incline, by normal adhesion alone, loads comparable to those taken up by the Fell locomotives. Use of the central rail for ascending the incline was abandoned.

The central rail remained in use, however, for braking trains on the way down. It survived incorporation of the Cantagallo into the Leopoldina Railway, and narrowing of the gauge to one metre. New locomotives equipped with steam-operated Fell brakes were ordered from North British Locomotive Co. in 1928 and again as late as 1944. Two noted British railway enthusiasts, in a book published in 1966[84], described the Fell locomotives used on the incline as having extra horizontal driving wheels to grip the centre rail: sadly, they were mistaken. By then, the point was academic, for the line had closed in 1965.

That the Fell system could in fact be advantageous, practical and reliable, uphill as well as down over a long period, was eventually demonstrated by the Rimutaka Incline in New Zealand.

Lessons from the earlier Fell railways were evidently absorbed by the engineer-in-chief responsible for the line, John Carruthers. The ruling gradient was kept to 1 in 15, the minimum curve to 5 chains radius. The running rails on the incline were steel, 70 lb per yard, compared with 53 lb on adjoining sections. The incline was about three miles long.

Fell himself does not seem to have been directly involved, although the 'Mr Hemans' who attended the Goathland trials[85] was probably the Hemans of consulting engineers Hemans & Bruce, who advised on design of the Rimutaka locomotives. Four locomotives were built by Avonside Engine Company Ltd in 1875: they were designed by Avonside's chief draughtsman H. W. Widmark. Two similar locomotives followed from Neilson & Co. in 1886. They were 0-4-2Ts with radial boxes to the trailing axle; two outside cylinders powered the vertical wheels and two inside cylinders, side by side, powered the horizontal wheels. These were driven by rods from the inside cylinder on their side of the locomotive, and coupled across it by gears. The horizontal wheels were pressed against the central rail by strong springs, tightened up by right- and left-handed screws. The working steam pressure was 120 lb per sq. inch., soon increased to 150 lb and later to 160 lb. Weighing nearly 40 tons in working order of which 32 tons was on the driving wheels, and with a pressure of some 30 tons available on the central rail, one of these locomotives could take a load of 65 tons up the incline.

The Rimutaka Incline was opened for traffic in 1878, and was operated until 1955 when a 5½ -mile long diversionary tunnel was completed. The Fell locomotives remained in use as long as the incline itself, and outlived various adhesion-only locomotives drafted in to assist. On closure, the first of the Fell locomotives, no. 199 *Mont Cenis* was preserved.

In designing a big robust high-powered locomotive with the drive to the central rail simplified as much as possible, Widmark and the New Zealand railways' engineers had evidently hit on a winning combination. But it was not the final development in central rail locomotive design to take practical form.

This came early in the twentieth century with improvements made by M. Hanscotte, engineer at the Fives-Lille company[86]. Hanscotte allowed some lateral displacement of the cradles carrying the horizontal wheels,

so that passage of curves or faults in the central rail could be made without damage of the sort which had occurred at Mont Cenis. Springs to press these wheels against the central rail were replaced by compressed air mechanisms, the pressure being regulated according to gradient and weight of train. This meant that the horizontal wheels could be placed at the ends of a locomotive, where they were driven by chains and bevel gears from the outermost axle of the vertical wheels.

Hanscotte had solved the problem of how to design a two-cylinder central-rail locomotive - admittedly using technology which had not been available to the pioneers.

After experimental installation on an electric tramway at La Bourboule, Auvergne, in 1904, the Hanscotte system was used for a metre gauge steam line from Clermont Ferrand to the summit of the mountain called Puy de Dôme: the summit station was at an altitude of 1,415 metres (4,642 feet). There were two long lengths where the central rail was installed; the ruling gradient was 1 in 8.33 (i.e., 120 mm per metre) and the final ascent of the mountain was at this gradient continuously for some 5 km (3 miles). The sharpest curves were 40 metres radius (about 2 chains). Five 0-6-0T locomotives incorporating the layout described above were built by Fives-Lille during 1905-6, and the *Chemin de Fer du Puy de Dôme* opened in 1907.

Evidently the Hanscotte system was a success, for during the First World War the railway attracted the attention of the military authorities. In 1917 all five locomotives were requisitioned: they were then used to shunt rail-mounted artillery into elevated locations. With them had gone much of the track. But requisitioned equipment was returned to Clermont Ferrand by 1920, and the railway was rebuilt and re-opened, in 1923.

Now, however, there was a bus service parallelling the lower part of the route, and traffic on the upper section was dependent on the weather, cloudy or clear: the railway tended to be either under-used or over-stretched. About 1925 it occurred to the company that it would do better to dismantle its railway and convert the trackbed into a toll

THE MONT CENIS FELL RAILWAY

AUVERGNE. - Le Tramway au pied du Puy de Dôme

*Last application of the central rail system to ascent of steep gradients, and a successful one technically, was the Puy de Dôme Railway opened in 1907. Here the train will shortly engage the central rail and ascend by a corkscrew route to the top of the mountain in the background: course of the line near the summit can be seen.*

**Le dernier en date construit avec un système de rail central pour l'ascension des pentes taides, le Chemin de Fer du Puy de Dôme, ouvert en 1907, fut le meilleur du point de vue technique. Ici le train va bientôt s'engager sur le rail central et montera en spirale jusqu'au sommet de la montagne qu'on voit au loin. Le trace de la ligne est visible près du sommet.**

AUTHOR'S COLLECTION.

road: this was done, and from 1926 tourists were taken to the summit of Puy de Dôme not by train but by snub-nosed Renault charabancs.

Four of the locomotives were bought by Etablissements Poliet & Chausson for their cement works in Cher département and used on a steeply graded line laid in 1925 between quarry and works. That sounds as though the central rail was laid, or at least intended. But this is uncertain and as Keith Clingan (to whom I am indebted for this information) points out, in railway history assumptions can be very dangerous. The locomotives were scrapped only about 1950.

There was another application of the Hanscotte system in France, it was used between 1907 and 1911 on a steeply-graded mineral branch of the metre gauge *Chemin de Fer de Provence*: Hanscotte horizontal wheels were added at the rear only of a 0-6-0T to increase the load it could haul.

Early in 1895 J. B. Fell himself had taken out another central rail patent, no. 762. This

covered drive by electric motors rather than steam. The same year the Snaefell Mountain Railway was built in the Isle of Man. Fell's son G. Noble Fell was engineer, the 3 feet 6 inches gauge was used, with electric traction, and the central rail was installed. But it was used, and still is, only to provide lateral stability, on a line with many exposed locations, and for braking on the descent[87]. Electric cars with all axles powered ascend the 1 in 12 gradient by normal adhesion alone.

In France, the PLM opened its metre gauge Chamonix line in stages between 1901 and 1908 with electric traction. It included gradients as steep as 1 in 11.11 (40 mm in 1 metre); on these a central rail was installed, but once again only for braking[88] (despite its supposed use for adhesion by another British writer who should have known better[89]). New passenger trains which did not require the central rail were introduced in 1958; it continued in use for some years for the old stock.

In 1910 and 1914 New Zealand Railways

217    *Chemin de fer du PUY DE DOME. — Passage à la Grande Tranchée.*    *ND. Phot.*

built two colliery branches near Greymouth, to Roa and to Rewanui, with ruling gradients of 1 in 25 and 1 in 26 respectively. On both of these the Fell central rail was installed to brake downhill trains, and lasted until 1966[90].

In the Isle of Man, the Manx Northern Railway's 0-6-0T *Caledonia* had been used to power works trains during construction of the Snaefell Mountain Railway. It was taken back again to operate over the top section of the line in celebration of its centenary in 1995: and for this it was fitted with brakes, both hand and hydraulically-operated, to work on the central rail[91].

As well as the Fell railways which were completed there were, as with railways of all types, many others proposed but not built; likewise, many layouts for central rail locomotives were suggested as improvements on those actually constructed. The engineering press in the late 1860s was replete with the latter. Fell himself in 1889 spoke confidently[92] of a new layout for two cylinder locomotives, which were to be used on a line

proposed to run from Oulx, near Bardonèccia, over the Col de Montgenève to Briançon. In 1903, the Ansaldo company of Genoa got as far as building a central rail locomotive intended for military railways, and ran it on an experimental line near Rome.

It is clear that the Fell railway did not carry all before it, as had seemed likely in the heady days of the late 1860s when *The Times* for instance had forecast a period 'when every mountain range in Europe shall be traversed by its "Fell's Railway"'[93].

There were really two reasons for this. Firstly, it soon became clear that adhesion locomotives could take trains of useful weight up steeper inclines than had been supposed. This was found to be so of locomotives of conventional design - particularly in dry conditions - but more so of multi-wheeled locomotives with some flexibility of wheelbase to enable them to traverse sharp curves. Such locomotives were developed in great variety, notably by Fairlie, Meyer and

*The Puy de Dôme Railway's central rail is clearly seen in this picture of a descending train.*

**Le rail central du Chemin de Fer du Puy de Dôme est bien visible sur cette gravure d'un train descendant.**

79

Mallet, but J. A. Longridge had ideas in this direction too, which the curious will find described in patents nos. 3,259 of 1872 and 15,773 of 1884.

The second reason was the rapid development of mountain rack railways. Sylvester Marsh had applied in 1858 for a charter to build a rack railway to the summit of Mount Washington, New Hampshire. After several years of experiments with models and attempts to raise funds, he had a 600-ft demonstration line running over part of the proposed route by 1866. The first stage of the permanent line, the Mount Washington Cog Railway, was opened in August 1868, a couple of months after the Mont Cenis Railway, and the line was opened to the summit in July 1869.

Reports of the success of the Mount Washington railway enabled Niklaus Riggenbach, who had taken out a French patent for a rack railway in 1863, to obtain in April 1869 a concession to build one up the Rigi mountain in Switzerland. This was opened in May 1871 and was an immediate success. By the end of the decade there were at least eight Riggenbach rack railways in operation. Riggenbach's ladder rack with individual rungs was much improved by his associate Roman Abt, who in 1882 patented a rack with its teeth machined from bar. This was first used in 1884 and became the usual form of rack, to the extent that by 1929 some 72 Abt rack railways had been built throughout the world. When in the mid-1880s John Carruthers, who had originated the use of the Fell system at Rimutaka, recommended use of the Fell system on the Trincheras Incline of the Puerto Cabello & Valencia Railway in Venezuela, he was over-ruled by the consulting engineer in favour of the Abt rack: and he later said he agreed with the decision[94].

His principal reason was that drive by rack and pinion eliminated one of the Fell system's undesirable features, the friction in the journals which resulted from pressing the horizontal wheels against the central rail. Furthermore, where drive could be by rack and pinion alone, as it was at Trincheras, any problem of coupling pinions, or horizontal wheels, with the vertical adhesion wheels was eliminated.

Rack railways could also be (although many were not) built up gradients as steep as 1 in 4. Clearly this was far steeper than any line worked by normal adhesion which was no competitor. On a rack railway, however, friction between pinion and rack became substantial on sharp curves (it was no problem at Trincheras where the sharpest curve was $7\frac{1}{2}$ chains radius). A Fell railway could pass round sharper curves than a rack railway - though probably not by very much. It is evident also that it needed less precision in laying than a rack railway. Both systems could and did aid secure braking of descending trains, but the Fell system also offered lateral security, which the rack did not. With one exception: when Eduard Locher designed a rack system for the steepest rack railway of all, up Mount Pilatus with gradients almost as steep as 1 in 2 upon which a normal pinion would climb out of the rack, he used a rack with teeth both sides and horizontal[95] pinions. This seems to combine the best features of both systems, and it would be interesting to know whether the inventor was influenced by knowledge of the Fell system.

The rapid spread of the rack railway was no doubt also a consequence of the strong marketing efforts of Riggenbach and then Abt, who had big incentives in the strong protection afforded by their patents. Although the rack system itself was old, a patent on a particular form of rack and drive must have been difficult to evade; but however many detailed layouts for central rail drive were patented by Fell, it looks as though there were other people designing still more layouts which would evade his patents. Even if Fell successfully instigated construction of a mountain railway on the central rail system, there was no guarantee he would benefit from patent royalties.

One gets the impression that Fell decided to exploit, if not as an alternative, then equally, the central rail's second important characteristic: lateral stability. As early as 1868 he took out a patent for monorail, supported on trestles, in which the vehicles would be stabilised by horizontal rollers: by 1870 this scheme had evolved into a railway of very narrow gauge, from 6 inches to 1 foot 6 inches, still supported on trestles and with trains stabilised by horizontal rollers outside and below the level of the carrying-rails. It too was patented and would, he supposed, be of particular value to the military authorities, since such a line could be built quickly from standardised components with minimal earthworks. One was built, demonstrated and, for a time, used at Aldershot in 1872[96].

By then however Fell was being attracted more by the continuous trestle aspect and less by lateral stability. In reconstructing the Pentewan Railway to 2 feet 6 inches gauge in 1873-4 he evidently hoped to build extension lines on continuous trestle of varying height, avoiding so far as possible the need for cutting and embankment. The lines were not constructed, although a suitable locomotive was. He got his opportunity as engineer to the Torrington & Marland Railway (1880), 3 feet gauge, where there were long and, in places, high timber viaducts built partly in place of embankments. Once again they were patented and their standardised design and ingenious use of timber seem to hark back to Fell's early experience in the timber business.

In his ventures Fell found loyal support in the person of Edmund Barnes. Barnes was present at the trials of the Cantagallo locomotive at Goathland, he drove the locomotive *Ariel* at Aldershot, and he supervised reconstruction of the Pentewan Railway.

What happened to other people involved in the Mont Cenis Railway? Both Tyler and Brunlees were eventually knighted: Tyler in 1877 following a successful term of office as Chief Inspector of Railways, Brunlees in 1886 following completion of the Mersey Railway with its tunnel, for which he was joint engineer. Both men, and Crampton too, were closely involved in the proposals for a Channel Tunnel in the 1870s and 1880s.

Brogden's firm, John Brogden & Sons, contracted for some 200 miles of railways in New Zealand in 1871 and 1873, although these did not, apparently, include the Rimutaka Incline. Sir Edward Blount remained chairman of the Western Railway of France for 30 years, until 1894.

The Duke of Sutherland evidently made it his business, so far as railways were concerned, to exercise influence rather than wealth directly. He took up few railway directorships: he was to be found, rather, hosting the Russian Imperial Commission which inspected the Festiniog Railway in 1870, leading the members of the Indian Gauge Committee to inspect the 3 feet 6 inches gauge railways in Norway later the same year, presiding over a meeting held at his London house in 1873 to consider a remarkable proposal to increase trade with the Far East by presenting a railway to the Emperor of China. A happy exception was his chairmanship of the Isle of Man Railway Company from 1872 to 1879, seeing it through from financing and construction to profitable operation.

Lord Abinger reappears in railway history in the 1880s[97]. Having reached the rank of lieutenant general, he retired to Inverlochy Castle, near Fort William. Here he in due course became the first chairman of the West Highland Railway Company. On 23 October 1889 he cut, ceremonially, the first sod. A surviving photograph shows him dapper in mutton chop whiskers and grey bowler, with a slightly portly appearance which confirms the uncertainty in family legend as to whether his nickname 'Puffing Billy' derived from his figure or his interest in railways.

In the upper Maurienne, the consequence of the opening of the Mont Cenis Tunnel was near-collapse of the economy. Many of the inhabitants left for Canada or Argentina. Lanslebourg, which had had 6,671 inhabitants in 1860, was down to 5,639 by 1873. No other railway ever linked it to the outside world. Lanslebourg was however served by bus as early as 1910, when a service was instituted between Modane and Susa over the Mont Cenis. The First World War put a stop to this pioneering effort, but subsequently there were bus services up the road on the Italian side,

*Susa station, 1995. Assuming that the proposed layout in the plan on page 47 was built, Mont Cenis trains terminated in the foreground, having approached from behind the photographer's left shoulder. The long and narrow shed, left, which now has rail tracks on both sides but limited road access, appears to occupy the site of the customs shed (Magasin de la Douane) shown in the plan: might it be the original building?*

**La gare de Suse, 1995. En supposant que le plan de la page 47 fut réalisé, les trains du Mont Cenis arrivaient à gauche de l'épaule du photographe et terminaient leur course au premier plan. Le hangar long et étroit à gauche, auquel on accède par des voies ferrées de chaque côté, mais d'accès difficile par la route, semble occuper l'emplacement du 'Magasin de la Douane' visible sur le plan. Est-ce peut-être le bâtiment d'origine?**
AUTHOR.

and Lanslebourg more remarkably was linked to Modane by a rural electric trolleybus.

With the growth of road traffic, a car-carrying shuttle train service was instituted through the Mont Cenis Tunnel in 1953. It proved its worth, particularly in winter, until the equivalent road tunnel was opened in 1980.

On the pass itself, in the aftermath of the second world war the frontier was moved several miles to the east. This enabled the French to make use of the possibilities of hydro-electric power offered by the region and the resultant scheme, completed in 1970, involved incorporating the little lake of Mont Cenis into a much larger reservoir which inundated the course of the railway across the plateau.

The Fell railway was never entirely forgotten, and in 1968 there were centenary celebrations in Susa. In 1961 an article in *The Railway Magazine* drew attention to the survival of some of its tunnels and avalanche shelters[98] and the opportunity for the author to go to see for himself, accompanied by his wife and son, arose in August 1995. The *Fédération des Amis des Chemins de Fer Secondaires* kindly put me in touch with a French enthusiast, Monsieur J-B Lemoine, who was able to confirm that there

was indeed still something to see.

On leaving Chambéry, there appeared ahead a seemingly solid wall of mountains but the valley of the Arc eventually proved to twist and turn its way between them. Fort L'Esseillon was as prominent in view as it was to travellers on the MCR. It may well be that diligent research would reveal traces of the railway along this stretch of road, although we were unable to find the big loop at Termignon, and the prominent remains were beyond Lanslebourg.[99]

From Lanslebourg the road zig-zagged upwards through the pine forests, just as it did in Mont Cenis Railway days. The hairpin bends showed clear traces of the railway, where even a two-chain curve was not sufficient to follow the road. At the first hairpin the curve of the roadway had been enlarged into the mountainside, which was supported by a masonry retaining wall, and the third hairpin was similar. At the second hairpin, and likewise at the fourth and fifth, the mountainside was too steep for this: from the apex of the bend, a short curving cutting led to the entrance of a tunnel, which continued the curve and brought the railway back to daylight and the roadside a hundred yards or so uphill. The condition of these tunnels, and of the avalanche shelters described below, had deteriorated to the point that in most cases it was evidently unsafe, or at least risky, to enter.

Having achieved the col we were well above the tree line. All round, steep grassy slopes led up to high rocky mountains. The old road headed down to the water's edge of the reservoir which has submerged most of the plateau. The new continued inevitably at a higher level: this had the advantage of bringing us by car to pretty much the viewpoint on the hillside of Whymper's engraving which appears as an illustration on page 51. Past the dam now, the road descended by new zig-zags to join up with the old ones. It did so near the point at which the railway diverged from the road to follow the older road which had been abandoned because of avalanches. Here appeared what a sign described as Tunnel Fell: it was, in fact, a very substantial masonry avalanche shelter, complete with portal at one end - the other has collapsed - built on top of a stone arch bridge over a stream. The course of the railway, descending along the mountainsides at 1 in 14, could clearly be distinguished to the point a mile or more ahead where it re-joined the road.

Across the frontier into Italy the descent began: the same panorama met our eyes that had so delighted travellers by train; the same rapid increase in fertility and successive changes in vegetation while we descended as they had down and down, lower and lower, to arrive at Susa baking in the North Italian sunshine.

The station seemed a good place for which to head. It was still open, even though it has been since 1871 in effect the terminus of a four-mile branch. Exploration produced a most unlikely goods shed, long and narrow with tracks both sides but limited road access, all of which suggested it might have originated as a transhipment shed between narrow and standard gauge. Much later I discovered the plan, reproduced on page 47, which confirms that (if proposals were carried out) it was indeed on the correct site.

We headed back up the hill, stopping to examine many surviving traces of the railway which we had noticed in passing earlier: earthworks, bridges, tunnels and avalanche shelters, the latter with openings in the side for, presumably, light and release of smoke. Some, clearly, had received a certain amount of maintenance subsequent to closure of the railway: but whether to support the hillside, or

*One of many of the Fell railway's avalanche shelters which in 1995 still survive beside the road from Susa up to Mont Cenis.*
**Un de nombreux bâtiments du Chemin de Fer du Mont Cenis, servant d'abri contre les avalanches, existe encore près de la route qui mène de Suse au Mont Cenis.**
AUTHOR.

*In Susa, J. B. Fell is not forgotten: street name opposite the station, 1995.*
**A Suse, J. B. Fell n'est pas oublié: cette rue, en face de la gare, porte son nom, 1995.**
AUTHOR.

to provide a very narrow emergency route in event of avalanche, I have been unable to find out. I would not vouch for their present day condition. In this brief visit we noticed traces of the railway at some 22 locations between Susa and Lanslebourg, and there are certainly more to be found. Pieri in *La Ferrovia del Moncenisio* notes 25.

On a knoll above the reservoir stood *La Salle Historique du Mont Cenis*, a small museum open, according to the green Michelin guide *Alpes du Nord*, only in July and August. The prize exhibit was an ornate tail lamp, once used on MCR trains. It was accompanied by a display of pictures of the railway, and of the passage of Mont Cenis down the ages.

We continued, down the zig-zags to Lanslebourg; second gear stuff all the way, even downhill, and a reminder, once again, of just how audacious a concept was the Mont Cenis Railway.

Earlier had come one of those strange coincidences which occasionally arise when one is seeking knowledge of some particular subject. Endeavouring to park in car-crowded Susa, I turned into a side street opposite the station and immediately found a shady spot. We had arrived, according to the sign which we now saw for the first time, in the *Via John Barraclough Fell, ingegnere, 1815-1902.*

# ACKNOWLEDGEMENTS

I am particularly grateful to F. Keith Pearson, who has willingly and generously exchanged information with me while working himself on his own much more extensive projected book about Fell and his mountain railways.

I am grateful to the Countess of Sutherland for permission to photograph and reproduce documents in the Sutherland records at Staffordshire Record Office.

The photographs and drawings of MCR equipment as subsequently employed on the LE and LEB Railways (see pp. 5, 8, 63, 64, 71 and 72) appeared first in *Voies Etroites de la Campagne Vaudoise. Chemin de Fer Lausanne-Echallens-Bercher: Cinquante Ans de Traction Electrique*, mentioned in the bibliography, is an extract from this, and I am grateful to those who prepared these books (G. Hadorn, J.-L. Rochaix, M. Grandguillaume, S. Jarne, A. Rochaix and F. Ramstein) for their permission for the further reproduction of this material here.

Many others have helped too. I am most grateful to Lord Abinger, Keith Clingan (Industrial Railway Society), Margaret Ecclestone (Alpine Club Library), Roger Fouret, U. Gachet (CF LEB), Ronald D. Grant, R. F. B. Greig (translator), Jean-Bernard Lemoine, Ben Longridge, Michael Longridge of Usk, Michael Longridge of W. Yorks, the Rev'd R. N. Longridge, Nicholas R. Mays (News International), Michael Messenger, Keith Moore (IME), Melvyn K. Rees (Patent Office), Michel Sirop, and the staffs of Birmingham Central Library, British Library, Flintshire County Record Office, Mitchell Library Glasgow, Musées d'Art et d'Histoire de Chambéry, National Library of Scotland, National Railway Museum, The Post Office Archives and Record Services, Public Record Office, The Royal Commission on Historical Manuscripts and Staffordshire Record Office. My wife Elisabeth and son Hugh provided help and support during our exploration of Mont Cenis.

# SOURCES & BIBLIOGRAPHY

## ARCHIVES

**Post Office Archives:**
file Post 29, Piece no. 131.

**Public Record Office,** files:
BT31/1223/282c: Centre Rail Locomotive & Railway Co. Ltd.
BT31/1222/2820c: Mont Cenis Railway Co. Ltd.
BT31/1351/3634: The Patent Centre Rail Co. Ltd.

**Staffordshire Record Office:**
Papers of the 3rd Duke of Sutherland concerning the Mont Cenis Railway, refs. D/593/P/27/1/1, D/593/P/27/1/2 (includes *Report of James Brunlees Esq. C.E. to the Concessionary Company* 1865).
Henry Wright's in-letters ref. D593/Q/2/1/1, Mont Cenis Railway bundle (Wright was the duke's private secretary).

## PUBLICATIONS

Allen, C. J., *Switzerland's Amazing Railways* revised edition 1965
Bellet, J., *Le Col du Mont-Cenis: 'Porte Millenaire des Alpes'* St Jean de Maurienne, 1976
Bellet, J. and others, *Mont Cenis, porte des Alpes* Chambéry 1989
*Bradshaw's Shareholders' Guide...* 1861-2
*Bradshaw's Railway Manual...* 1863-71
Bray, D., *Cog Railway* Mt Washington 1991
Buckley, R. J. *A History of Tramways* 1975
*Chemins de Fer Regionaux et Urbains*: no. 100, 1970 (early narrow gauge locomotives); no. 106, 1971 (Rigi); no. 141, 1977 (Chamonix); no. 231, 1992 (MCR p. 48); no. 256, 1996 (Puy-de-Dôme)
Colburn, Z., *Locomotive Engineering* 1871
Coleman, T., *The Railway Navvies* 1968.
Cottrell, P. L., 'Railway Finance and the Crisis of 1866...' *Journal of Transport History* Feb.1975
Couche, C., *Voie, Matériel Roulant et Exploitation Technique des Chemins de Fer* c.1871
Dendy Marshall, C. F., revised Kidner, R. W., *A History of the Southern Railway* 1963
Desbrière, T. M. A., *Études sur la Locomotion au moyen du Rail Central...* Paris 1865
*Dictionary of National Biography*

*The Engineer* 1865-72 (frequent references)
*Engineering* 1866-75 (frequent references)
Fell, J. B., '*Locomotive Engines and Carriages on the Centre Rail System...*', paper to the British Association, reproduced in *The Engineer* 31 Aug. 1866 pp. 156-8
Fell, J. B., '*The Application of the Centre Rail System to a Railway in Brazil...*', paper to the British Association, Ulverston 1870
Foray, F., *Franchir les Alpes* Chambéry 1992
Grant, R. 'J. B. Fell's Centre Rail Locomotives', *Locomotives International* nos. 22 & 23, 1993-4
*Guide de Tourisme Michelin: Alpes du Nord*  Paris 1994
Hadorn, G., & others, *Chemin de Fer Lausanne-Echallens-Bercher: Cinquante Ans de Traction Electrique* Lausanne 1986
Hearder, H., & Waley, D. P., *A Short History of Italy* Cambridge 1963
Helps, A., *Life and labours of Mr Brassey 1805-1870* 1872
Hibbert, C., *The Grand Tour* 1987
*Illustrated London News* 10 Feb. 1866, 1 Feb. 1868
*Industrial Past* summer 1979 (Crampton)
*Institution of Civil Engineers, Minutes of Proceedings:*
   Tyler, H. W., 'On the Working of Steep Gradients and Sharp Curves on Railways' 1867
      Carruthers, J., and others, 'Railway Steep Inclines' 1889
      Longridge, J., in vol. LXIII 1880-1, p 94;
      Vignoles, C.B., in vol. XXIX 1869-70 p. 301;
      Memoirs (Obituaries): Brassey, T.; Brunlees, J.; Buddicom, W. B.; Fell, J. B.; Jopling C. M.; Jopling, J.; Longridge J. A.; Sutherland, 3rd Duke of.
Kalla-Bishop, P. M., *Italian Railways* Newton Abbot 1971
Leitch, D. B., *Railways of New Zealand* Newton Abbot 1972
Lewis, M. J. T., *The Pentewan Railway* Truro 1981
Longridge, R. N., *The Longridge Tale* Exeter 1991
Lowe, J. W., *British Steam Locomotive Builders* Cambridge 1975
Lunn, A., *Mountain Jubilee* 1943 (chapter XVIII 'Edward Whymper')
Marshall, J., A *Biographical Dictionary of Railway Engineers* Newton Abbot 1978
Marshall, J., *The Cromford & High Peak Railway* Halifax 1996
Messenger, M. J., *North Devon Clay* Truro 1982
Mitchell, J., *Reminiscences of My Life in the Highlands* 1971.
Morris O. J., *Snowdon Mountain Railway* 1960
*Newcomen Society, Transactions of the*, vol XXXVI 1963-4 pp. 127-8 (Mont Cenis Tunnel)

Palluel-Guillard, A., *Impressions de voyage en Savoie...* Chambéry 1990

Pearson, F. K., *Snaefell Mountain Railway 1895-1970* 1970

Pendred, V., 'On the Adhesion of Locomotive Engines and Certain Expedients for increasing or supplementing that function', *Transactions of the Society of Engineers* 1865. That part of the text referring to central rail locomotives was reprinted in *The Engineer* 17 Nov. 1865 but without the plates of MCR locomotives included in the *Transactions*.

Pieri, E., *La Ferrovia del Moncenisio...* Susa 1996

*Railway Magazine* Feb. 1956 (Rimutaka)

Reid, S. J., (ed) *Memoirs of Sir Edward Blount KCB* 1902

Reynolds, D. H. B., 'The Mont Cenis Fell Railway in 1960', *Railway Magazine* June 1961

*Rimutaka Tunnel Official Opening Ceremony* 1955 (New Zealand Railways booklet)

Roney, Sir C. P., *Rambles on Railways* 1868

Roney, Sir C. P., *The Alps and the Eastern Mails* 1867

Rush, R. W., *The Furness Railway 1843-1923* 1973

Smiles, R., *Memoir of the late John Brogden* Barrow-in-Furness 1872

Stenton, M., *Who's Who of British Members of Parliament* vol. I 1832-1885, 1976 (entries for Brogden A., Smith J.)

Thomas, J., *The West Highland Railway* 1971.

*The Times* 1861-72 (frequent references)

Tyler, H. W., *REPORT from Captain Tyler, R.E., to Her Majesty's Postmaster General, of his recent Inspection of the Railways and Ports of Italy...* PP vol. XL, 1866

Tyler, H. W., *REPORT of Captain Tyler, R.E., to the Board of Trade, on the RAILWAY proposed by Messrs. Brassey & Co. for Crossing the MONT CENIS,...* PP vol. L, 1865; reproduced also in *Engineering* 23 June 1865 and *The Times* 29 June 1865

Tyler, M. L., ed. Seymour, M., 'Captain Tyler, R. E.: A Memoir by his daughter', *Festiniog Railway Magazine* no. 30, 1965

Wade, E. A., 'The Patent Narrow Gauge Railways of John Barraclough Fell', special issue of *The Narrow Gauge* 1986.

Whitehouse, P. B., & Allen, P., *Round the World on the Narrow Gauge* 1966

Whymper, E., *Scrambles amongst the Alps in the years 1860-69,* 2nd edition, 1871

# REFERENCES

Abbreviations:
MPICE  Minutes of Proceedings of the Institution of Civil Engineers
POA      Post Office Archives
StaffsRO Staffordshire Record Office

1  Roney 1868
2  *Bradshaw* 1861, p.333.
3  Roney 1868, appendix 3, which also contains an outline of the development of postal services with the Far East.
4  Buckley 1975 p.9.
5  Fell's paper was printed in *The Engineer* 31 Aug 1866.
6  Letter by Charles Fox to *The Times* 10 Aug 1865.
7  *Engineering* 3 Aug. 1867 p.223.
8  *The Engineer* 31 Aug. 1866 p.156.
9  Cottrell 1975 covers admirably the financial background to railway construction at this period.
10  StaffsRO D593/Q/2/1/1.
11  Dendy Marshall 1963 pp.332-42.
12  *The Times* 9 Mar. 1865
13  POA ref. POST 29/131, item *Programme…for the Locomotive Trials….*
14  Mitchell 1971.
15  Bellet 1976
16  Coleman 1968.
17  According to Fell, in *The Engineer* 31 Aug. 1866 p 156; Roney 1868 gives 1 May 1866 as the date of commencement of works.
18  MPICE vol. XXVI (1867) p.341.
19  PP vol. XL, 1866; the original hand-written report, with drawings, survives in POA, ref. POST 29/131.
20  MPICE vol. XXVI (1867) p.328.
21  This report, and much else relating to construction of the railway, are contained in StaffsRO ref. D593/P/27/1/1 Guard Book.
22  According to Couche 1871 (p.707) who gives the figure as '0 m 267'; Roney 1868 (p.351) writes 'the top of the centre rail…is 9 inches higher than the outer or ordinary rails' and the same figure appears in *The Engineer* 8 Nov 1867 p.399.
23  *Alpine Journal* vol. IV, May 1868, p.61.
24  StaffsRO ref. D593/P/27/1/1 Guard Book contains ms copy of Tyler's third report on the MCR.

25  StaffsRO ref. D593/P/27/1/1 Guard Book.
26  MPICE vol. LXIII, 1880-1 pt 1, p.125
27  *Engineering* 19 June 1868 p.599.
28  *The Engineer* 19 June 1868 p.449.
29  Fell, paper to the British Association, Sept. 1870.
30  *The Times* 6 May 1868.
31  *The Times* 9 May 1868.
32  StaffsRO ref. D593/P/24/4 (A57).
33  *The Times* 26 May 1868.
34  *Morning Post* 28 May 1868.
35  *Engineering* 19 & 26 June 1868.
36  see the author's *Narrow Gauge Steam…*pp.41-6.
37  *The Times* 16 June 1868; *Engineering* 19 June 1868 pp.596 & 599; *Engineering* gives the departure time as 6.30 am, but from comparison with other reports of the initial timetable in eg *The Times* 19 June 1868 it is clear that *Engineering* was giving French time which was 50 mins. behind Italian time.
38  Balance sheet, 31 Oct. 1868, StaffsRO, ref. D593/Q/2/1/1.
39  The description of the route is based principally on: MCR timing diagram, StaffsRO ref. D593/P/27/1/2; *The Engineer* 8 Nov. 1867; *The Times* 25 May 1868; *Engineering* 19 & 26 June 1868; plans enclosed with Tyler's report of 19 July 1867 to PMG, POA ref. POST 29/131; Roney 1868; and Whymper 1871.
40  *The Times* 22 June 1868.
41  *Engineering* 26 June 1868.
42  *The Times* 29 Sept. & 27 Nov. 1868; see also *The Engineer* 29 Sept. 1871 p.212.
43  Copy letter, StaffsRO, ref. D593/P/27/1/2.
44  *Engineering* 27 Nov. 1868 p.481; *The Engineer* 25 Sept. 1868, pp. 233, 237.
45  *The Times* 18 & 25 Nov. 1868.
46  *Engineering* 27 Nov. 1868 p.481.
47  MPICE vol. XXXV 1872-3 p.337.
48  *The Engineer* 6 Oct. 1871 p.234; Bellet 1976, p.121.
49  *The Engineer* 29 Sept. 1871 p.212.
50  MPICE vol. LXIII 1880-1 part I, p.95.
51  *The Engineer* 6 Oct. 1871 p.233 footnote; the tunnel has subsequently been lengthened, and then shortened again: see *Transactions of the Newcomen Society* vol. XXXVI p.128.
52  *The Illustrated London News* 10 Feb. 1866 p.146.

53 Bellet 1976
54 *Engineering* 28 June 1872 p.430.
55 Descriptions of no. 1 appear in *The Engineer* 17 Nov. 1865 p.317, & 31 Aug. 1866 p.156; *Engineering* 5 Jan. 1866 p.7; Tyler's 1865 report to the Board of Trade; Desbrière 1865; Pendred 1865; Couche 1871 p.709.
56 MPICE vol. XXVI 1867 p.314.
57 *The Engineer* 30 June 1865 p.408.
58 Descriptions of no. 2 appear in *The Engineer* 17 Nov. 1865 p.317, & 31 Aug. 1866 p.157; *Engineering* 5 Jan. 1866 p.7; Tyler's 1865 report to the Board of Trade; Tyler, MPICE vol. XXVI 1867 p.314; Pendred 1865; Couche 1871 p.709.
59 *The Engineer* 31 Aug 1866, p.160.
60 *The Engineer* 31 Aug 1866, p.157.
61 *The Engineer* 18 Sept 1868, pp 215-6 & supplement; 25 Sept 1868 pp, 233, 237 & 240.
62 *Engineering* 19 June 1868 p.599.
63 *Engineering* 19 June 1868 p.599
64 Paper read to the British Association at Liverpool, Sept. 1870.
65 MPICE 1889 p.156.
66 *Engineering* 27 Nov. 1868 p.481.
67 The following details are derived principally from Couche 1871, pp.712-5.
68 Couche 1871, p.718
69 Longridge, MPICE vol. LXIII, 1880-1, p.97.
70 *The Engineer* 28 January 1870 p.54.
71 Details of the numbering system and of the subsequent history of MCR carriages and wagons which went to the LE are largely derived from Hadorn 1986.
72 Dimensions as in *Engineering* 19 June 1868 p.599. Slightly different figures are given elsewhere.
73 *Engineering* 17 May 1867 p.497.
74 *The Times* 18 Aug. 1868.
75 *Engineering* 19 June 1868 p.599.
76 MPICE vol. XXVI 1867 pp 340-3; *The Engineer* 25 Sept. 868 pp.233, 237.
77 Hadorn 1986 pp.32 & 116; *Railway Magazine* June 1961 p.402.
78 Couche 1871 p.715.
79 MPICE vol. LXIII 1880-1 pt 1, p.97.
80 Bergeron, MPICE vol. LXIII 1880-1 pt 1, p.94; *Engineering* 19 June 1868 p.599.
81 *Engineering* 28 June 1872 p.429.
82 *The Railway Gazette* 14 June 1935.
83 *The Engineer* 6 October 1871.
84 Whitehouse & Allen 1966
85 *Engineering* 28 June 1872 p.429.
86 *Chemins de Fer Régionaux et Urbains* no. 256, 1996, pp.3-11 & 24-5.
87 Pearson 1970.
88 *Chemins de Fer Régionaux et Urbains* no. 141, 1977.
89 Allen 1965 p.78.
90 Leitch 1972 pp.81-3.
91 *Railway Magazine*, Feb 1995 p.58; June 1995 p.37; Aug. 1995 p.39; Nov. 1995 p.41.
92 MPICE 1889 p.156.
93 *The Times* 26 May 1868 p.6.
94 MPICE 1889 pp.125, 129.
95 i.e., at right angles to the carrying wheels.
96 Fell's developing ideas for narrow gauge railways on trestle or semi-continuous viaduct are well covered by: Wade 1986; Lewis 1981; Messenger 1982.
97 Correspondence between the present Lord Abinger and the author; Thomas 1971.
98 Reynolds, D. B. H., 'The Mont Cenis Fell Railway in 1960' *The Railway Magazine* June 1961.
99 For the benefit of anyone planning to repeat this excursion, the whole area is covered by Michelin 1:200,000 map sheet 244, Rhône-Alpes.

# INDEX

LONGITUDINAL SECTION.

GROUND PLAN.